THE FLEA

by James Fritz

The Flea was first performed at The Yard Theatre,
London, on 11 October 2023.

THE FLEA

by James Fritz

CAST
Connor Finch | Arthur Somerset and Henry Newlove
Norah Lopez Holden | Queen Victoria and Emily Swinscow
Scott Karim | Abberline, Hammond and Gladstone
Séamus McLean Ross | Charlie Swinscow and Bertie
Prince of Wales
Sonny Poon Tip | Hanks, Barwell and Euston

CREATIVE AND PRODUCTION TEAM
James Fritz | Writer
Jay Miller | Director and Dramaturg
Naomi Kuyck-Cohen | Set Designer
Lambdog1066 | Costume Designer
Dominique Hamilton | Hair and Make-Up Designer
Josh Anio Grigg | Sound Designer
Jonathan Chan | Lighting Designer
Gino Ricardo Green | Video and Projection Designer
Sung Im Her | Movement Director
Jatinder Chera | Casting Director
Jimmy Justice | Assistant Director
Frances Heap | Costume Assistant
Wabriya King | Production Dramatherapist
Rachel Coffey | Voice Coach
Jennifer Taillefer | Production Manager
Julia Nimmo | Company Stage Manager
Laura Dewhirst | Assistant Stage Manager
Callum Harris | Set Carpenter
Felix Villiers | Prop Fabricator
Scott James | Props Supervisor

BIOGRAPHIES

Connor Finch

Connor Finch plays Arthur Somerset and Henry Newlove. He trained at Guildhall School of Music and Drama. *The Flea* is his professional stage debut.

Connor's breakthrough screen role was as Street in the hugely successful BBC TV adaptation of Dolly Alderton's *Everything I Know About Love*. Other screen credits include ITV's *Professor T* and *The Larkin*.

Norah Lopez Holden

Norah Lopez Holden plays Queen Victoria and Emily Swinscow. Norah's previous stage appearances include *The Art of Illusion* (Hampstead); *Hamlet* (Young Vic); *Equus* (Theatre Royal Stratford East); *The Winter's Tale/Eyam* (Shakespeare's Globe); *The Almighty Sometimes* and *Our Town* (Royal Exchange, Manchester); *Ghosts* (HOME, Manchester); and *Epic Love and Pop Songs* (Pleasance, Edinburgh). On radio, she has appeared in *Our Friends in the North*, and other productions for BBC Radio 4.

Scott Karim

Scott Karim plays Abberline, Hammond and Gladstone. He recently wrapped a sold-out West End run of *2:22 A Ghost Story* (Lyric Theatre) opposite Cheryl Cole. His other credits include *Chasing Hares* (Young Vic); *The Invisible Hand* (Kiln Theatre); *Great Britain* and *Othello* (National Theatre); *Oklahoma!* and *The Country Wife* (Chichester Festival Theatre); *The Arrival* and *The Invisible* (Bush Theatre); *The Village* (Theatre Royal Stratford East) and *Young Marx* (Bridge Theatre).

Scott is currently in *HALO* for Paramount+. Other television credits include *Dracula* and *The Dumping Ground* (BBC); *The Great* (Hulu); *Electric Dreams: Crazy Diamond* (Channel 4) and *Britannia* (Sky).

Séamus McLean Ross

Séamus McLean Ross plays Charlie Swinscow and Bertie Prince of Wales. He trained at Guildhall School of Music and Drama. *The Flea* is his professional stage debut. At Guildhall, some credits include *Road* directed by Paul Foster, *Julius Caesar* directed by Anna Morrissey and *Either*, directed by Paapa Essiedu. Screen credits include ITV's *Payback* and Eleventh Hour's *Rebus*.

Sonny Poon Tip

Sonny Poon Tip plays Hanks, Barwell and Euston. Sonny trained with the National Youth Theatre Rep Company. He played regular Leo Bloom in the latest series of *Industry* for BBC and HBO. Most recently, Sonny has wrapped on a TBA Disney+ series. Other TV credits include *Halo* (Paramount+); *Holby City* (BBC); *Intruder* (Channel 5); *Professor T* (ITV); and *Anatomy of a Scandal* (Netflix). His theatre credits: *Three Sisters* (Almeida Theatre), directed by Rebecca Frecknall.

James Fritz

James Fritz is a playwright from South London.

Plays for stage include *Cashmoney Now* (The Big House); *Lava* (Fifth Word/Soho Theatre); *The Fall* (National Youth Theatre/Southwark Playhouse); *Parliament Square* (Royal Exchange/Bush Theatre); *Start Swimming* (Young Vic); *Ross & Rachel* (Assembly/BAC/59E59); *Four Minutes Twelve Seconds* (Hampstead Theatre/Trafalgar Studios) and *LINES* (Rosemary Branch Theatre).

Plays for audio include *The Test Batsman's Room at the End of the World*, *Dear Harry Kane, Eight Point Nine Nine*, *Death of a Cosmonaut, Comment Is Free* (all BBC Radio 4) and *Skyscraper Lullaby* (Audible Originals)

He has won the Critics' Circle Theatre Award for Most Promising Playwright, A Bruntwood Prize for Playwriting, The Imison and Tinniswood BBC Audio Drama Awards and the ARIA Radio Academy Award for Best Drama on two separate occasions. He has also been nominated for the Olivier Award for Outstanding Achievement in an Affiliate Theatre and was runner-up in the 2013 Verity Bargate Award.

Jay Miller

Director Jay Miller is the theatre director who founded The Yard Theatre and has been the driving force behind the organisation since its inception. Jay's credits at The Yard have included *This Beautiful Future* by Rita Kalnejais (★★★★★ The Stage), *The Crucible* (★★★★★ *The Sunday Times*, *Evening Standard*) and *Dirty Crusty* by Clare Barron (★★★★★ *Evening Standard*).

Naomi Kuyck-Cohen

Naomi Kuyck-Cohen is an interdisciplinary designer, working primarily in performance and installation, and has a practice co-designing set, costume, lighting, and spaces with Joshua Gadsby.

Designs include *I, Joan* (Shakespeare's Globe); *The Chairs* (Co-Design with Cécile Trémolières – Almeida Theatre); *FORGE*

(Barbican/MAYK/Transform Leeds); *in a word* (Young Vic); *The Greatest Play in the History of the World* (Royal Exchange/ Traverse Theatre/Trafalgar Studios); *BODIES* (Unlimited); *Nightclubbing* (The Lowry/CPT/tour); *OUT* (The Curve/The Yard/ tour); *Amsterdam* (ATC/Orange Tree/Theatre Royal Plymouth); *The Tyler Sisters* (Hampstead Theatre); *Cosi fan Tutte* (Longborough Opera); *Trigger Warning* (Tate Modern/tour); *FEAST* (Battersea Arts Centre/tour).

Co-designs with Joshua Gadsby include *There Is A Light That Never Goes Out* (Royal Exchange); *Trainers, or the brutal unpleasant atmosphere of this most disagreeable season* (Gate Theatre); *The Extinction Trilogy* (Hester Stefan Chillingworth); *Trap Street* (New Diorama/Schaubühne); *Dinomania* (New Diorama); *The Winston Machine* (New Diorama/tour); *We Should Definitely Have More Dancing* (Oldham Coliseum); NDT Broadgate; New Diorama's café and public spaces.

Josh Anio Grigg

Josh Anio Grigg is an artist, sound designer, and music producer who studied Drama, Theatre and Performance at Roehampton University, London. His recent works include *The Confessions*, (Volkstheater, Vienna, 2023); *IV* (The Yard Theatre, London, 2023); *Inchoate Buzz* (Tramway, Glasgow, 2023); *Love* (Park Avenue Armory, New York, 2023); and *Live to Tell* (Camden People's Theatre, London, 2023). Grigg lives and works in London.

Jonathan Chan

Jonathan Chan trained at the Guildhall School of Music and Drama. His credits include *Grindr: The Opera* (Union); *Snowflakes* (Park Theatre/Old Red Lion); *All Roads* (London Tour); *Get Happy* (Pleasance); *Emmeline* (UK Tour); *In the Net* (Jermyn Street); *Grandad Me and Teddy Too* (Polka); *The Solid Life of Sugar Water* (Orange Tree); *Heroin to Hero* (Edinburgh Fringe); *Move Fast and Break Things* (Camden People's Theatre/Edinburgh Fringe); *Pussycat In Memory of Darkness* and *The Straw Chair* (Finborough); *Maybe Probably* and *Belvedere* (Old Red Lion); *Different Owners at Sunrise* (The Roundhouse); *Barstools to Broadway,* Amphibian (King's Head); *Sticks & Stones, Time* and *Random* (Tristan Bates); *Urinetown: the Musical* and *Opera Makers* (Guildhall School); *Fidelio* (Glyndebourne – Assistant Lighting Designer) and *The Passenger* R&D (Guildhall – Associate Lighting Designer).

Gino Ricardo Green

Gino Ricardo Green is a director and video/projection designer. He is a co-founder of Black Apron Entertainment.

Credits as Video/Projection Designer include *Tambo and Bones* (Theatre Royal Stratford East); *August In England* and *Lava* (Bush Theatre)*; Othello* (NT, Co-Video Designer); *The Ballad of St John's Car Park* (Icon Theatre); *Treason: The Musical in Concert* (West End); *That is Not Who I Am* (Royal Court Theatre); *Kabul Goes Pop: Music Television Afghanistan* (Brixton House/HighTide); *Edge* (NYT); *Children's Children* (Director of Photography/Editor – ETT)*; Beyond The Canon* and *Poor Connection* (RADA); *Sweat* (Donmar Warehouse/West End); *Passages: A Windrush Celebration* (Black Apron at the Royal Court); *Hashtag Lightie* (Arcola Theatre); *Lightie* (Gate Theatre).

Credits as Associate Video/Projection Designer include *Small Island* (National Theatre); *Get Up Stand Up! The Bob Marley Musical* (West End) and *Be More Chill* (The Other Palace/West End).

Sung Im Her

Sung Im Her (Seoul, South Korea) obtained a master's degree in contemporary dance at Hansung University. In 2004, she moved to Brussels, Belgium to study at P.A.R.T.S., the acclaimed contemporary dance school led by Anne Teresa De Keersmaeker.

After graduating in 2006, she started working with Jan Fabre/ Troubleyn, Les ballets C de la B and Needcompany in Belgium.

In parallel Sung Im Her has been creating works of her own, starting with *Philia* (2012), *En-trance* (2013), *Tuning* (2014) and *You Are Okay!* (2016). She moved to London in 2016.

In 2019, she created two new works: *NUTCRUSHER* and *W.A.Y.* Both works were commissioned by the Korean Arts Council and premiered at the renowned ARKO Arts Theater in Seoul. With *NUTCRUSHER* she was elected by the Korean Arts Council as Best Emerging Artist of 2019. *NUTCRUSHER* was also selected for Aerowaves '21 and in 2022 was a part of Horizon showcase, presented during the Edinburgh Fringe Festival where she received a five-star review by *The Skinny*. In 2021, Sung Im Her's dance piece *W.A.Y* (re-work) premiered at The Place in London and received a four-star review by the *Guardian*.

Last year, Sung Im Her created *Everything Falls Dramatic* for Korean National Contemporary Dance Company and toured in Seoul, Madrid, Brussels, Manchester and London. Sung Im Her received the Dance Artist of the Year in 2022 by the Korean Ministry of Culture and was recently named as one of ten 'Stage sensations to watch out for in 2023' by the *Guardian*.

Lambdog1066

Lambdog1066 is amateur couture. A legacy frothing at the mouth, speaking in gilded tongues, embroidered under the cleft hoof and between the needle's eye; a legacy scantily clad. From lavish throws to pig lewd costumes, every stone fard with nicotine contour.

Lambdog1066 was the costume designer for *TOM* by BULLYACHE (The Yard Theatre). Other credits include *Lonely Cowgirl,* which was nominated for Best Wardrobe/Styling at the UK Music Video Awards 2021 and *Sissy Fatigue,* which received Best Music Video at Thunderdance Film Festival 2019.

Dominique Hamilton

Theatre credits include *Carousel, Aida, Satyagraha, Iolathe, A Midsummer Night's Dream* (English National Opera); *Bat out of Hell* (London Coliseum); Swing Work with Garsington Opera, *Little Shop of Horrors* (Regent's Park Open Air Theatre); *42nd Street* (Theatre Royal Drury Lane); *Fairview* (Young Vic Theatre); *Oklahoma!* (Young Vic Theatre); *Bagdad Café* (Old Vic Theatre); *Wuthering Heights* (Wise Children in association with the Old Vic, Bristol Old Vic and National Theatre); *Harry Potter and the Cursed Child* (Palace Theatre); *Mandela* (Young Vic Theatre); *Secret Life of Bees* (Almeida Theatre); *A Strange Loop* (Barbican Theatre).

Films include: As Hair and Make-up Designer: *Unremarkable (2017), A Fragile Life (2019), Lessons (2020), Home Safe (2022)* (short films by Sam Seccombe Films). As Crowd Hair and Make-up Artist: *Matilda* (2022), *Wicked* (2024).

Jimmy Justice

Jimmy Justice is an emerging director and artistic practitioner with over half a decade of working in the theatre industry and community arts facilitation and a graduate of East 15's Theatre Directing MA. Their work often platforms and amplifies trans, neurodivergent and working-class stories and voices and advocates for political and social action in response to issues that these communities face.

Alongside freelancing as a director and dramaturg, Jimmy is currently working on adapting Ovid's *Metamorphoses* into an original play that speaks to issues surrounding contemporary issues of transness and power structures in gendered relationships with support from Arts Council England and running the popular cabaret event *CRABS!* at The Glory in Haggerston.

They have independently created and produced several immersive theatrical shows with the performance collective HalliGalli, including a successful Edinburgh Fringe run at The Tolbooth Market in 2018. As co-creator of F-CLUB, a collective of queer Northern cabaret artists, Jimmy has produced events attended by artists worldwide, including Taiwan, Malaysia, Canada, U.S.A. Canada and performed live at international events, including Seztkasten Wien collective (Austria) and in danceswithcircles collective's cabaret (America). Their performance artwork has been exhibited twice at Leeds Arts Gallery (A-Z, 2018; Sonic Bodies, 2019).

Stemming from a background that straddles classical theatrical training and community arts leadership, Jimmy is cultivating a creative practice that aims to be simultaneously brave and challenging in its artistic statement and nurturing and empowering to the communities that it serves.

Jatinder Chera

Jatinder Chera took a position at the Royal National Theatre, following his graduation from the Casting Certificate, at the National Film and Television School. Prior to this, he worked as an actor, having trained at Millennium Performing Arts.

For the Bush, Jatinder has cast Olivier Award winning *The P Word*, *A Playlist for the Revolution*, and *Sleepova*. Further credits include *The Nutcracker* (Bristol Old Vic); *Up Next Gala 2022* (Lyttelton Theatre, NT); and *A Family Business* (Staatstheater Mainz/UK Tour).

As a Casting Associate at the National Theatre, he worked on *The Father and the Assassin* (Olivier Theatre).

As Casting Assistant at the National Theatre, Jatinder worked on *Othello*, and *Much Ado About Nothing* (Lyttelton Theatre), *Small Island* (Olivier Theatre), and *Trouble in Mind* (Dorfman Theatre).

Jennifer Taillefer

Jennifer Taillefer is a freelance production manager and has worked across theatre and live events in both the UK and North America. Recent credits include *Grease: The Live Experience* (Secret Cinema); *Of Mice and Men* (Birmingham Rep/Leeds Playhouse); *Pinocchio*, *Get Dressed*, *The Bolds*, *Anansi the Spider*, *Maggot Moon* (Unicorn Theatre); *The Wonderful World of Dissocia* (Theatre Royal Stratford East); *Dirty Dancing* (Secret Cinema); *The Comedy of Errors*, *London Road* and *Grand Hotel* (Mountview). She also works as a designer most recently on *Scrunch* (Unicorn Theatre). When not working on shows, Jennifer runs performing arts-specific Carbon Literacy training across the UK, helping theatres to address their carbon footprint and develop their sustainability goals.

Wabriya King

Recent theatre includes *Beautiful Thing* and *Tambo & Bones* (Theatre Royal Stratford East); *A Strange Loop* (Barbican Centre); *School Girls; Or, The African Mean Girls Play* (Lyric Hammersmith); Matthew Bourne's *Romeo & Juliet* (New Adventures); *August In England* (Bush Theatre); *Julius Caesar, Falkland Sound, The Empress* and *Cowbois* (RSC); *Romeo and Juliet* and *Secret Life of Bees* (Almeida Theatre); *For Black Boys Who Have Considered Suicide When The Hue Gets Too Heavy* (New Diorama Theatre/ Royal Court/West End); *Drive Your Plow Over the Bones of the Dead* (Complicité); *Blue* (ENO); *Further than the Furthest Thing* (Young Vic); *Family Tree* (Actors Touring Company); *Bootycandy* (Gate Theatre); *Blues for an Alabama Sky* (National Theatre); and *Hamilton* (West End).

Film includes: *Empire of Light; Chevalier.*

Rachel Coffey

The Flea marks Rachel's fourth production at The Yard having previously been the voice coach on *Athena*, dir. Grace Gummer: *Armadillo*, dir. Sara Joyce and also *The Crucible*, dir. Jay Miller.

Currently Rachel is also coaching on Arcola's world premiere of *Gentlemen*, dir. Richard Speir and also recently *The Misandrist* dir. Bethany Pitts.

Rachel's twelve years of experience as a professional voice and dialect coach spans theatre, TV, new media and film. She has coached actors in productions with the Royal Court, Birmingham Rep, Liverpool Everyman, Sheffield Crucible, Theatre by the Lake, along with various West End productions and national tours. In film and TV Rachel has coached actors in productions for BBC, ITV, Channel 4, Netflix, Disney, Amazon and Warner Brothers amongst others. Recent work includes the upcoming feature film *Freud's Last Stand* for Sony Pictures, the expectant Ubisoft gaming release *Skull and Bones* and the new BBC drama *The Reckoning.*

Rachel trained in Voice (MA) at Royal Birmingham Conservatoire, in association with the RSC and in Acting (BA) at the Arden School of Theatre/Manchester University. Rachel also enjoys a long association with the NYT.

Julia Nimmo

Julia Nimmo trained in Design for Theatre & Television at Charles Stuart University, Wagga Wagga, Australia and was awarded 'Individual Stage Manager of the Year' at the SMA National Stage Manager Awards 2019.

Stage Manager theatre credits include *Recognition* (Talawa Theatre Company); *A Proper Ordinary Miracle* (National Theatre Wales); *A Midsummer Night's Dream* and *The Tempest* (Guildford Shakespeare Company); *an unfinished man* (The Yard Theatre); *Run It Back* (Talawa Theatre Company); *Buffering...* (Palace Youth Company/Watford Palace Theatre); *Queer Lives* (Historical Royal Palaces, Tower of London); *Rust* and *The Trick* (HighTide/Bush Theatre); *Songlines* (HighTide/Dugout Theatre); *Paper. Scissors. Stone.* (Tara Finney Productions); *Frankie Vah* (Paul Jellis Ltd); *All the Things I Lied About* (Paul Jellis Ltd/Katie Bonna); *Harrogate* (HighTide/Royal Court Theatre); *This Much* (Moving Dust); *Flare Path* (Birdsong Productions/Original Theatre); *Lampedusa* (HighTide/Soho Theatre); *Beached* (Marlowe Theatre/Soho Theatre); *The One* (Soho Theatre); *The Real Thing* (English Touring Theatre); *Macbeth* (Wildfire Productions, Cell Block Theatre, Sydney); *The Beauty Queen of Leenane* (Wildfire Productions, Seymour Centre, Sydney).

Laura Dewhirst

Laura is a theatre technician who has performed an array of backstage jobs, but mainly focuses on stage management.

SM credits include *Doktor Kaboom and the Wheel of Even More Science* (Something For The Weekend, Edinburgh Fringe Festival); *Seance* (Darkfield, Edinburgh Fringe Festival)

DSM credits include *Cat and Mouse* and *Doubtful. Hapless. Guests.* (SMU Productions).

TSM credits include *Berlusconi* (FMP Productions, Southwark Playhouse).

ASM credits include *The Woman in Black* (PW Productions, Fortune Theatre); *The Seagull* (Jamie Lloyd Company, Harold Pinter); *A Christmas Carol...ish* (Berks Nest LTD, Soho Theatre); *The Swell* (Damsel Productions, The Orange Tree Theatre); *Tony!* (The Tony Blaire Rock Opera, Edinburgh Fringe Festival)

Stage crew credits include *Noises Off* (Theatre Royal Bath, The Phoenix Theatre); and *The Ocean at the End of the Lane* (National Theatre, Duke of York's Theatre).

Wardrobe credits include *Silence* (Donmar Productions, Tara Theatre).

Props credits include *Allegiance* (New Wolf Productions, Charring Cross Theatre).

'The Yard Theatre is a mecca for some of the most interesting theatre in Britain.' *British Vogue*

The Yard reimagines theatre. Our programme crosses genres and breaks boundaries, because the artists we work with want to say something new, in new ways. We work with artists who reflect the diversity of East London, who tell new stories. They invite us into journeys of escape, euphoria, possibility and hope. Through this, The Yard reimagines the world.

We've developed artists like Michaela Coel, Alexander Zeldin, Marikiscrycrycry and Dipo Baruwa-Etti, and nightlife collectives like INFERNO and Pxssy Palace. They've all used their vision and energy to give us new stories and narratives for what the world could be.

Recent work includes: ★★★★★ *An unfinished man* written by Dipo Baruwa-Etti, directed by Taio Lawson (2022), *The Cherry Orchard*, reimagined by Vinay Patel, directed by James Macdonald (2022), ★★★★★ *The Crucible* written by Arthur Miller, directed by Jay Miller (2019), ★★★★★ *Dirty Crusty* written by Clare Barron, directed by Jay Miller (2019), ★★★★ *Armadillo* written by Sarah Kosar, directed by Sara Joyce (2020), ★★★★ *A New and Better You* by Joe Harbot, directed by Cheryl Gallacher (2018) and ★★★★★ *Buggy Baby* by Josh Azouz, directed by Ned Bennett (2018).

THE FLEA

James Fritz

Acknowledgements

This one took a long time and needed a lot of help, so bear with me. Deep breath:

Mum, for teaching me the 'Rattlin' Bog' song when I was little and giving me my structure.

Tom Martin, Simon Longman, Vinay Patel, Phoebe-Eclair Powell, Emily Wraith and of course Tamara Moore for either reading it, being bored by me talking about it or both.

Michael Gould, who helped make Abberline. Elmi Rashid Elmi and Terique Jarrett who helped make Charlie. David Moorst, who helped make Somerset and Newlove. Oliver Coopersmith who helped make Euston, Barwell and Hanks. Sophie Duvel, Kayla Meikle and Rebekah Murrell who helped make Emily and Victoria.

Norah, Seamus, Connor, Sonny and Scott for breathing such life into all of them. A company of five with the force of a hundred.

Naomi, Jordan, Dom, Gino, Sung Im, Josh, Jonathan, Jatinder, Jenn, Julia and Laura for picking up the play and making something so mad and beautiful with it. I hope if anyone else picks it up they do the same.

Jimmy Justice, for your brilliant mind.

All of the historians whose work I have learnt from and butchered, too many to list. The true story of Cleveland Street is a fascinating subject and anyone interested should go on a proper deep dive and absolutely not trust anything in this play.

Anthony Simpson-Pike, Ashleigh Wheeler, Johanna Taylor, Lara Tyselling, Katherine Igoe-Ewer, Kia Noakes and everyone else at The Yard Theatre who fed back, organised workshops and otherwise helped me sort this mad thing out over many years. I got it wrong a lot of times. Thanks for sticking with it.

God, The Yard is a special place for me. Once upon a time
I pulled a lot of pints there. I had a lot of lock-ins. I met the love
of my life.

And then, years later, I got to come back.

So thank you, Jay Miller, for being a good boss back in the day,
and a great friend and collaborator now. You built this play from
the ground up, and it's yours as well as mine.

J.F.

'The flea on the feather and the feather on the wing and the wing on the bird and the bird in the nest and the nest on the twig and the twig on the branch and the branch on the limb and the limb on the tree and the tree in the bog and the bog down in the valley-o.'

'The Rattlin' Bog', old Irish folk song

Characters

EMILY SWINSCOW
FLEA
RAT
HORSE
CHARLIE SWINSCOW
PETER GREGG
HENRY NEWLOVE
FRED ABBERLINE
COMMISSIONER
LORD ARTHUR SOMERSET
EARL OF EUSTON
CONSTABLE HANKS
GEORGE BARWELL
CHARLES HAMMOND
MR BLACK
BERTIE, PRINCE OF WALES
QUEEN VICTORIA
GOD ALMIGHTY
MAGGOT
WILLIAM GLADSTONE

And DELIVERY BOYS, POSTMASTERS, ANGELS

Note on Text

A line with no full stop at the end indicates an unfinished thought.
A line with a dash at the end indicates an interruption.
A forward slash indicates where the next line comes in.

This text went to press before the end of rehearsals and so may differ slightly from the play as performed.

Prologue

A small Bermondsey tenement.

The kitchen.

It's been well lived in.

EMILY SWINSCOW *cleans up. She's tired.*

A stove.

A pot.

Some ingredients. Onions. A stick of butter. Some carrots.
EMILY *chops and puts them in the pot. Meat and stock. A low heat. She watches it come to the boil.*

EMILY (*to us*). Time in the pan.

S'all it needs.

Pause. She watches it bubble.

Just gotta wait.

She waits. For quite a while.

We wait with her.

We keep waiting.

The meat cooks. And then, eventually…

We'll start with the flea.

'Cause it's as good a place as any.

Truth be told when it comes to the tragedy of Emily Swinscow there's a hundred places could serve as the beginning, but we'll start with the flea and see how we get on.

Pause.

So there's this flea.

Right, and I want you to imagine like, we see it right up close, it's giant it's enormous it's this

This horrible fuckin giant

Flea.

And if by some miracle this flea could somehow speak English he'd be saying something like

FLEA. Christ I'm thirsty.

EMILY. You know

FLEA. I'm absolutely gasping mate.

EMILY. And so Mr Flea leans back his head and he sinks his fangs into the fleshy back of this rat he's standing on

FLEA. Yum

EMILY. And he sucks sucks sucks up the blood and oh Lord Almighty he's never felt so good in his life he is overwhelmed with ecstasy every nerve in his tiny body is screaming pleasure pleasure pleasure

And we move up.

And now we see the rat, right?
There's Mr Rat and he's mangy, he's all bitten to shit by this fucking flea and he's scratchin and he's squealing and he's thinking

RAT. Ooh gosh that's itchy.

EMILY. You know

RAT. That is really bloody itchy actually

EMILY. And as the flea keeps biting, the little rat freaks and twitches and runs scratching scratching right into the eyeline of a horse…

HORSE. Neigh.

EMILY. Now this is a mean and nasty horse.
The sort of horse that has never felt love nor affection.
Never been stroked or given a juicy sweet apple on a hot

summer's day and as a result has grown into a real fucking prick of a horse.

Which means the only instinct it has when it's afraid is to lash out at something smaller than itself.

And so the flea bites the rat

RAT. Ow

EMILY. The rat spooks the horse

HORSE. Neigh!

EMILY. And the horse kicks the rat but it
Misses.

It misses.

And instead
Crack!

Its hoof connects with something hard and soft

VOICE. Oh God.

Someone

someone help oh God call a doctor!

EMILY. And just like that, the whole world changed.

ACT ONE

EMILY *in her kitchen.*

She checks the stew. Adds some salt.

EMILY (*calls*). Charlie!

Everything was fine up until it wasn't. That's the thing that would strike Emily Swinscow when she looked back.

Everything was fine right up until it wasn't.

The weekly outgoings of the Swinscow family in the summer of 1889 were

Seventeen shillings and fourpence

which was fine, since their income column boasted

Twenty shilling and six

and so the sums made sense.

Six shilling came from Emily herself, who knew how to work a sewing machine.

Twelve shilling, from Thomas, her husband, who worked as a tanner over at the Leathermarket.

It was good honest work that sadly meant he stank of the dogshit they used to treat the leather.

He smelt so bad, bless him, that as he walked by children would burst into tears and birds would fall from the sky.

But despite the stench, Emily loved him, because he was kind and fair and could make her laugh so hard it hurt her sides.

So,

Emily six shillings, Tom twelve shillings and

While it weren't much, a final two shillings and sixpence from their only son –

Her son enters. He's in a messenger uniform.

Charlie!

CHARLIE. What?

EMILY. Who delivered telegrams for the Royal Mail.

He investigates the stew.

Gimme your uniform

CHARLIE. Why?

EMILY. Because it's filthy.

CHARLIE. It's fine.

EMILY. I can smell it from   CHARLIE. It's my uniform it
here.   can smell how I like.

EMILY. I ain't gonna argue with you.

CHARLIE. Er I like to wear it this way this is the way I like to wear it. Besides, it won't dry in time.

EMILY. It will if I wash it   CHARLIE. What's cooking?
now.

CHARLIE. I'm starvin.

EMILY. It's not ready yet.

He investigates the stew.

Oi hands off you I said it ain't done so –

A violent thump thump thump on the door. She freezes.

Shhh.

CHARLIE. That Dad?

EMILY. He wouldn't knock. Go in the other room.

He doesn't move.

Go!

CHARLIE *leaves.*

There are few things more violent in this world than a knock on the door in the middle of the evening.

Thump thump thump. She opens the door.

PETER. Mrs Swinscow?

EMILY. Yes.

A man enters.

PETER. Name's Peter Gregg. I work down at the tanner's. I've come about your husband.

EMILY. He been arrested?

PETER. No ma'am.

EMILY. So, it's the other thing then.

He nods. Pause. She takes this in.

Dead. Okay.
How did… How did it

PETER. There was a rat.

EMILY. A rat?

PETER. A rat in a manner of speaking a rat spooked our horse and it kicked out just as your Thomas was bending down to pick up his knife and bless him he took a full kick to the head and that was that I'm afraid. No luck at all.

EMILY. Drunk?

PETER. Just tired.

I'm awful sorry. We're sort of friends me and him. I don't know if he talked about / me?

EMILY. No.

PETER. Well. We was friends.

Pause.

Well I'll leave you to your grief. Evening young man.

CHARLIE. Hullo.

PETER *leaves. Beat.*

Ma?

EMILY. Emily wished she could say that in that moment she was thinking happy thoughts of her husband. But none would come.

Instead just eight words rattled round her head.

Jesus

Christ

What we gonna do for money.

Pause.

CHARLIE. Should we drink to him.

EMILY. Later, maybe.

Pause.

So on we go.

***

Outside the General Post Office.

CHARLIE. Henry. Henry please

I know you're angry –

NEWLOVE. I ain't angry with you, Swinscow. I'm done with you.

CHARLIE. Don't say that.

NEWLOVE. Why should I talk to someone who says they're gonna meet at an appointed time and place and then doesn't have the common courtesy to show up?

Stood on that street corner like a fucking lemon, over an hour with people looking at me thinking who's that, who's that fucking lemon standing on his own, I don't like people thinking I'm a fucking lemon, Swinscow, because I ain't one.

If there's one thing you can say about Henry Newlove, it's that he's always right where he's sposed to be.

CHARLIE. Somethin happened

NEWLOVE. You don't think I have better ways to spend an hour? I paid for the room

CHARLIE. I wanted to come. I was thinking about it
About you

all day.

NEWLOVE. Course you were.

What was it? Better offer –
Or just bored of me?

CHARLIE. Nah. That ain't it. That ain't it at all.

NEWLOVE. Well it don't matter either way does it. Nice knowing you.

CHARLIE. Henry. My father died.

This stops NEWLOVE *in his tracks.*

He died and

I.

I really need your help.

***

EMILY. At the very same moment

Scotland Yard.

ABBERLINE. Twenty years.

EMILY. The Famous Detective, Fred Abberline

ABBERLINE. Twenty fucking years, Commissioner, please.

EMILY. The lead cop on the Whitechapel murders.
It had been almost a year since his face appeared on every newspaper
But he still heard the comments behind his back and now –

ABBERLINE. Twenty years on the job and that's it is it? Piss off. No thank you, good luck.

COMMISSIONER. Thank you. Good luck.

> You must have known this was coming. There has never been a case like Whitechapel in the history of this police force. Of course scrutiny was going to be applied to every decision –

ABBERLINE. I did the best I could.

COMMISSIONER. No one's doubting that.

ABBERLINE. I'd like to see anyone else –

COMMISSIONER. But Detective Moore's report clearly shows that some grave procedural errors were made and that those errors –

ABBERLINE. Sir –

COMMISSIONER. Those errors led to the killer escaping custody.

ABBERLINE. This report. It's gonna be made public?

COMMISSIONER. I wouldn't worry yourself.

ABBERLINE. Please.

> I'll be a laughing stock, sir. If this goes public I'll be a national fucking joke.

***

EMILY. At the very same moment.

A private dining room.

Lord Arthur Somerset

SOMERSET. I can't believe this.

EMILY. The third and least-loved son of the Eighth Duke of Beaufort

SOMERSET. I really can't believe this

EMILY. Had just sat down for dinner with his best friend Henry Fitzroy, Earl of Euston

EUSTON. Don't make a fuss.

SOMERSET. No fuss he says!
Sits there and tells me he's got someone new on the go and expects me not to need to know everything.

EUSTON. I shouldn't.

SOMERSET. Come on…

EUSTON. I really –

SOMERSET. At least tell me who it is? Fitz, let me live vicariously.

EUSTON. Alright. (*Beat*.) It's William.

SOMERSET. William Merrigold or William, Phillipa's cousin?!

EUSTON. William, Phillipa's cousin.

SOMERSET. I knew it!

EUSTON. You never knew

SOMERSET. I mean obviously I didn't know but in a way I sort of did.

EUSTON. You're ridiculous.

SOMERSET. I'm jealous.

I'm seething with jealousy. Do you see?

EUSTON. It's nice.

SOMERSET. So come on then.
How long –

EUSTON. Six months.

SOMERSET. SIX MONTHS!

EUSTON. Keep your voice down.

SOMERSET. And you're only just telling me?

Well?

What's he like?

EUSTON. You've met him.

SOMERSET. No, but you know. What's he *like*.

EUSTON. I don't know. He's intelligent but not conceited. He's kind. He makes me laugh.

SOMERSET. Well, fuck you.

EUSTON. Truth be told.
I've never really felt like this about anyone.

Beat. Something about this wounds SOMERSET.

SOMERSET. Really?

EUSTON. Yes.

SOMERSET. So this isn't just a

EUSTON. No. No I don't think so.

Beat.

SOMERSET. Love?

EUSTON. Maybe, yes. Sounds silly but –

Beat.

SOMERSET. No, that's. That's wonderful. Fitz.

EUSTON. Yes.

SOMERSET. Really.

Beat.

Can I ask. Where do you go? The two of you.

EUSTON. Mostly, his mother's place.

SOMERSET. And that's –

EUSTON. Safe. Yes. Mercifully she understands.

SOMERSET. You can trust her? All it takes is a word –

EUSTON. She's his mother.

SOMERSET *lowers his voice*.

SOMERSET. You know Samuel Timothy was arrested

EUSTON. I heard.
>Turned in by his housekeeper.
>Walked in on them, apparently.
>Someone new every week.

SOMERSET. Which is why I worry when I hear that you're –

EUSTON. Arthur, you're sweet. It's safe. We're being careful.

>What about you? Any fresh hope?

SOMERSET. Chance would be a fine thing.

>Who has the time? The stables this time of year.

>But sometimes, I don't know –

>*Beat.*

>Can I

>I'd like to

>What does it feel like? With William. How is it different?

EUSTON. This one feels

>Like I'm batting at The Oval but every ball is underarm and every drive goes straight to the boundary.

>It's easy.

>Even though it's incredibly hard, everything feels easy.

>SOMERSET *takes this in.*

***

At the kitchen table, EMILY *counts some money painstakingly under her breath.*

It takes a while.

She finishes the count.

EMILY. Short. Again.

>*She gets up. Takes out a quarter-loaf of bread.*

>You must be hungry.

>*She smiles.* CHARLIE *breaks off a little bit. Eats. Looks at his mother. A beat. He puts the bread down.*

CHARLIE. I ate already. At work.

EMILY. Charlie.

CHARLIE. I ate already. Go on.

She looks at him. He pushes the bread towards her. She eats the bread. Tries not to show how hungry she is.

He watches her.

And then CHARLIE *puts money down on the table.*

EMILY. What's this?

CHARLIE. A bonus. They gave us a bonus at work for like being really good at deliverin telegrams, like they got this new thing where they give us bonuses for the best delivery boys and I won so –

She picks it up. Counts it.

EMILY. Charlie, you steal this?

CHARLIE. No –

EMILY. Where's it come from?

CHARLIE. Does it help?

Beat.

EMILY. Yeah. It helps.

CHARLIE. Then what's it matter.

He kisses her on the head. Leaves.

EMILY. Yeah

She should've asked more questions. Because that's what you do, innit, when your son comes home with mystery money, you ask all the questions, don't you?

And she meant to, but every time he came home with

CHARLIE. Another bonus

EMILY. She found herself saying

Thank you, instead.

Thank you, love.

She counts out the money again. She looks up. Can feel the judgement.

Safe lodging. A roof. They had it, and she didn't want to lose it. Not now.

It was less than a year since Whitechapel and she still had their names by heart. Every woman she knew did.

Polly. Annie. Liz. Catherine. Mary-Jane.

Five women.
All different.
All killed.
And the one thing in common?
A lack of safe lodging.

So yeah, she should have asked more questions. But she didn't.

Polly. Annie. Liz. Catherine. Mary-Jane.

CHARLIE *hands her a present.*

What's this!

CHARLIE. Happy birthday.

EMILY. That were weeks ago!

She tuts. Opens it. It's a beautiful plate. Willow pattern.

Oh the Willow pattern! Look at that.

CHARLIE. I remember you said whenever we pass the shop how pretty a thing it is and how you like the story yunnow

EMILY. Oh, it's such a sad story I love it. More crockery should tell stories I truly believe that.

CHARLIE. Yeah so I remembered and I thought well I hope I save enough in time for her birthday but I didn't quite manage which is why you're only getting it now so I'm sorry but –

EMILY. Love, this is –

I don't know what to say. No but really.

I'll put it pride of place.

CHARLIE. Well okay. Don't go on about it.

Pause. She beams at him.

EMILY. Tomorrow. When you get home.

I'm gonna treat us. Fuck it. Good steak chuck from the butcher on Tooley. We deserve it, eh.

The next night

She goes to check on the stew. It's still cooking.

She put the stew on.

And she laid the table.

And she waited for her son to come home

And she waited

Must be held up.

And she waited.

Be here in a minute

And she – how long do you wait 'fore you start to worry?

By midnight she was furious

By one she was worried

And by three her head was full up with thoughts of a future without him and she got down on her knees and she prayed to her God and she said

Lord

Please.

I keep picturing him dead down an alley somewhere, knifed in the gut, drowned in the Thames and I just think

Not him too you fucker you feckless thug not him too.

You took my Thomas and I didn't say nothing. I kept my counsel when there was lots I coulda said. Please don't take my boy as well.

Tell me what I can do to make him come home safe.

Tell me

Tell me

Tell me!

Sunrise.

And what with there being no sign of him and no word from the Almighty she got dressed and set out to find him herself.

The General Post Office. DELIVERY BOYS *and* POSTMASTERS *swarm around.*

Excuse me
I'm sorry have you seen
Do you know
I'm looking for –
Oi

I know you.

Henry. Henry Newlove.

NEWLOVE. Who's asking?

Beat.

EMILY. Charlie's mother.

NEWLOVE. I ain't seen him.

She punches him in the arm.

Ah fuck!

EMILY. Charlie didn't come home last night.

NEWLOVE. And what's that got to do with me?

She punches him again.

This is the Royal Mail. I'm an employee of the Crown!

EMILY. Don't gimme that. You ain't a fucking beefeater. You're a two-bit telegraph boy.

NEWLOVE. I'm a clerk –

EMILY. And you're all he talks about, you know that right? For months now, Henry this, Henry that, I'm meeting Henry

NEWLOVE. That's nice

EMILY. No it's pretty fucking boring actually but I humour it because I know how it is when you're that age and you like someone.

What I'm saying is

I know how much time you spend together, and I can't say it doesn't worry me but if he stayed at yours that's fine I just need to know because not coming home this ain't like him.

NEWLOVE. He weren't with me.

EMILY. Then where was he?

I know things about you boy, don't think I don't. I know things about you and if it comes to it I'll march into that office and start telling stories. Now, I don't want to do that I really don't. But this is my son and I'm worried that he's dead somewhere.

NEWLOVE. He ain't dead.

EMILY. Thank God.

NEWLOVE. He got nicked.

EMILY. I'll kill him.

What for.

NEWLOVE. Thieving. Someone broke into the office and stole the kitty.

This copper came to investigate saying

The day before.

HANKS. Uh, yes, right, hello everyone, um, okay listen please, listen, my name's – listen! – Constable Hanks, and I'm gonna need every one of you telegraph boys to empty your lockers. Please.

NEWLOVE. So he went along the line and when he got to Charlie's he found

HANKS. Fourteen shillings. Well well well –

CHARLIE. That's my money.

   I earnt it.

HANKS. How about this. If you can tell me where a telegraph boy earning two bob a week got fourteen shillings, well you can be on your way. But if not –

   EMILY *considers all this*.

EMILY. Fourteen shillings?
   Well. Shit. Okay.
   What station they take him to?

NEWLOVE. You see Charlie, you tell him to keep his mouth shut.

EMILY. His mouth shut?

NEWLOVE. I gotta get back to work.

EMILY. Henry. What station?

   NEWLOVE *stops*.

NEWLOVE. St Paul's.

***

A police station across town. A CONSTABLE *looking busy.*

EMILY. I'm looking for Constable Hanks.

HANKS. You've found him.

EMILY. Emily Swinscow. You picked up my boy Charlie yesterday.

HANKS. Right, yeah, the 'Great Post Office Robbery'

EMILY. He didn't steal nothing.

HANKS. Yes, that seems to be the case.

EMILY. I'm sorry?

HANKS. I know he didn't.

   Turns out after a bit of friendly questioning your boy told me exactly where he got that money, and you're absolutely spot on, it wasn't from robbing the Post Office.

EMILY. Oh…

Good.

HANKS. You seem surprised.

EMILY. No. I. No.

So you're gonna let him go?

HANKS. Yeah, no, 'fraid not.

EMILY. But you just said –

HANKS. I know what I said but even if he didn't steal the money I can't just let someone go when they've openly admitted to being on the game.

Pause.

EMILY. On the game?

What d'you mean on the game.

HANKS *finally looks up.*

HANKS. Oh. You didn't know.

EMILY. What you talking about?

She shakes her head.

HANKS. Shit.

Sorry.

Well, I hate to be the one to –

Charlie says that's where he –

He told me he'd been saving the money in his locker from his second job at a house where he spends time and I quote 'lying down with gentlemen upstairs'.

Beat.

Mrs Swinscow –

EMILY. Where is he?

HANKS. The station cells but

EMILY. Can I see him?

HANKS. That's not really

EMILY. Five minutes

HANKS. Possible.

EMILY. Please. You any children of your own Constable?

HANKS. I don't see how that's

>   Don't change the

EMILY. That's a yes, I take it? Bags under your eyes so they're still running the house ragged, what's that then, a two-year-old? Two-and-a-half?

>   Little boy is it?
>   No?
>   A little girl then. Bonnie little lass –

HANKS. Mrs Swinscow, please.

EMILY. Look. I'm asking nice. You seem like a decent sort.

>   If he's hauled 'fore the magistrate tomorrow he could be in Newgate by nightfall and then it might be a year or more till I see him.

>   Five minutes, that's all I'm asking.

***

The station cells. EMILY *sits across from* CHARLIE.

EMILY. You should've told me.

CHARLIE. Told you?

>   I thought you knew.

EMILY. Knew? How could I *know*? Charlie –

CHARLIE. I figured you just didn't want to talk about it –

EMILY. I didn't know. I / didn't.

CHARLIE. Alright. None of this was sposed to –

>   It was supposed to be safe. That's what Henry told me.

EMILY. Henry Newlove? From work?

CHARLIE. He told me everything would be safe and fine and so I didn't see the harm.

Henry's my mate, yunnow, he's been good to me since the day I got there, and we're close, you know, I've told you.

We're. Close.

Anyway, he came to me, he came to me a few months back and said Swinscow how'd you fancy earning a few extra quid and at the time I said, 'nah, no thank you', because we were getting by okay, but he said come to me if you ever change your mind.

But, course, then Dad died and the sums stopped working and I thought well, I can't let you take all of the burden of worrying, you know, I need to stand up, you know, help you out so I went to Henry and I said 'My father died, I need your help.' He said that he could get me a job at this house he works at sometimes uptown. He said that some of the other lads from the Telegraph Service all worked there. Ernie. George. Algernon.

I asked him what I'd have to do. And he told me. And I thought

Okay. Why not.

Even if it's only once or twice to get us to the end of the week.

So after work he takes me uptown to the house. And this place is nice, Mum, it is fancy, like nowhere I've ever been inside. Carpets and red furnishings and drapes and food like you've never tasted and I was surprised you know because if I'm honest I was expecting it to be kind've...

I met the fella who ran it and he said he liked the look of me and he thought I'd do well there and he gave me a tray of drinks and said go pass those out, so I did, and for a while that's all I had to do.

I walked round the rooms serving drinks to these men that were there. And a bit like the place the men were posh, and clean, and had those loud laughs that you hear from a mile off.

So I'm handing out drinks, and a few of them talk to me and I think okay, maybe this is all there is but then this fella says I'll give you a shilling if you come upstairs with me

And I needed a shilling.

And it went on like that.

I went to Henry and I said I didn't want to get into trouble. I know people are getting into trouble and he said that's the beauty of it. The police know all about this place. It's fine.

And then the Post Office got robbed and they thought it was me, but I figured it was alright to tell them where I got the money because the police were sposed to know about it, right. So I told the constable out there and he got all excited and put me in the cells which don't make no sense and now no one will listen to me.

I'm sorry Ma. I didn't mean

I didn't mean

I didn't mean to get into trouble.

***

The private dining room.

SOMERSET. Something's happened.

Something's happened and I've been dying to tell you about it.

EUSTON. I'm listening.

SOMERSET. I don't know how it happened I really don't but I think maybe I think I was inspired by sitting here listening to you talk about William and the way you seemed so…

EUSTON. Arthur

SOMERSET. I've met someone.

EUSTON. Oh.

SOMERSET. I think I might have met someone.

EUSTON. Really?

Good for you, Arthur. That's marvellous. Do I know them?

SOMERSET. I don't think so. It just happened. Just like they say, an arrow, a thunderbolt –

EUSTON. You're giddy.

SOMERSET. He's special. I don't know. And now

EUSTON. When did this happen?

SOMERSET. It's very new. But he's... it's...

I feel like I'm on opium or something I –

Don't laugh.

EUSTON. I'm not I –

SOMERSET. You are, you're laughing.

EUSTON. It's just.

I'm pleased for you. That's all.

Just. Don't get carried away.

SOMERSET. Too late.

EUSTON. And be careful. Am I allowed to know who it is?

SOMERSET. All will be revealed. I promise.

But I know that you're going to love them.

***

EMILY. Outside the police station

Emily Swinscow ducked into The Dog and Something and bought a pint of bitter she couldn't afford and thought

Fuck.

She thought

Fuck it!

She thought

Wouldn't it be great
Wouldn't it be fucking great to just
Give up.
You know?
Just down tools
Let whatever's gonna happen
Happen. Just this once.
Wouldn't that be blissful relief?

Beat. She finishes her pint.

But then, of course
She got to work.

GEORGE BARWELL, *MP, stands in the House of
Commons, mid-speech, whipping up the crowd.*

BARWELL. Mr Speaker, London is in the grip of a housing
crisis while this government sits on its hands!

While vast swathes of the city are misused by the aristocracy,
in my constituency of Bermondsey West living conditions for
the working poor are a disgrace!

Cholera and diphtheria run rife, while whole families live out
of a single room.

This house must agree that nothing effectual can be done for
the poor until their dwelling places are made decent and
wholesome!

Barwell's constituency office. Later.

EMILY. Mr Barwell!

BARWELL. Yes, Emily, isn't it? Emily –

EMILY. Swinscow, right you are sir, the memory on you what
a thing that is! You helped my Thomas with that dispute with
the council –

BARWELL. And how is dear Thomas?

EMILY. He's very dead sir.

BARWELL. I'm sorry to hear that.

EMILY. It's left me spinning round to stay still, truth be told.

But that ain't why I've come. Well, it is, and it isn't –

BARWELL. What can I do for you?

EMILY. These are lovely offices, sir, all this wood panelling
I feel like I'm up in court.

Something's happened with my son, something awful and
I thought who better to talk to than my local MP. I wanted

you to know how grateful we all are for the work you've
done in our neck of the woods sir, oh yes, the campaigning
on our behalf –

BARWELL. I only wish I could do more.

EMILY. The drinking water in our part of Bermondsey well it
ain't exactly clean but it's less brown than it was and that's
down to you and Mrs Barwell I truly believe that. Them new
gardens too

BARWELL. With the cherry trees? You like them?

EMILY. Oh yes, sir, just what the area needs, more cherry trees.

BARWELL. The blossom does catch the eye.

How's your living situation?

EMILY. We've been lucky. Got ourselves a decent little flat
these past few years, down on Tabard Gardens

BARWELL. I know the very ones.

EMILY. But with Thomas gone –

BARWELL. You're struggling to make rent.

EMILY. Yes, sir.

That's why I wanted to –

I wanted to come find you sir, because I think our interests
might be somewhat entwined. I know how you like to speak
up for the working man and my son well, he's a working
man and he's been rather done over if I do say myself.

BARWELL. Please. Start at the beginning. Tell me everything.

EMILY. And so she does.

Sparing no detail.

She tells the story of the horse and her husband and the rent
and her boy and his friend and a house in Fitzrovia and the
politician says things like

BARWELL. I see

EMILY. And

BARWELL. I am so sorry.

EMILY. And

BARWELL. What can I do to help?

> We can provide some support, and I know some very good people at the City Mission. Perhaps we can talk to your landlord and arrange a temporary freeze on the rent –

EMILY. That's all very kind sir but what I really need is for my boy to come home.

Beat.

BARWELL. Of course you do.

EMILY. I thought you could talk to someone. Get them to listen. He'll be sent down to Newgate prison if not and I can't have that. My favourite brother spent three years in Newgate and when he came out well he was half-human, sorry to say. It marmalised him. I can't have that happen to Charlie.

BARWELL. My dear. I sorely wish I could help, I do. But I'm afraid Charlie has confessed to a crime. Now you and I may not believe it should be a crime, but –

EMILY. Nah, I know, sir I understand that.

> But I thought

> Given your campaigning and such you'd be interested to know that

> The men Mr Barwell. At this place. Charlie says they weren't no ordinary men. They were gentlemen sir.

BARWELL. Gentlemen? What sort of gentlemen?

***

Scotland Yard. Abberline's office.

ABBERLINE. I can't deal with this now, George. It ain't a good time.

BARWELL. I've been doing a bit of digging into this woman's story and I think you should investigate.

ABBERLINE. Look –

BARWELL. Turns out this house in Fitzrovia is something of
an open secret in the right circles. Some of the rumours I'm
hearing –

ABBERLINE. Rumours, George that's all they –

BARWELL. Telegraph boys taken from their workplace to be
farmed out to rich aristocrats. Employees at all levels of the
Post Office involved. You must've heard of this place.

ABBERLINE. Everyone's heard of this place.

BARWELL. Then why haven't you investigated?

ABBERLINE. One. No one knows if it really exists. Two, if it
does no one knows where it is. And three. Why the fuck
would I?

BARWELL. The boy will be sent to Newgate

ABBERLINE. Then he should've made better decisions.
What do I care about some rent boy, George?
You know how many we arrest a week?

BARWELL. Charlie Swinscow is my constituent.

ABBERLINE. This is one of your campaigns.

BARWELL. I'll admit there's a certain poetry to the whole thing.
These are working-class lads, living on a knife edge. Lads
who took an honest job, and were blackmailed and
pressganged by their betters into something else. If that
doesn't sum up everything wrong with our country –

ABBERLINE. Save it for your pamphlets.

BARWELL. There is a good case to be made here. You know
that. Talk to the boy at least.

Beat.

ABBERLINE. Look, look into it if you want, that's your
business. But you'll have to find another detective. I'm retiring.

BARWELL. Retiring?

ABBERLINE. Done with the place. Got a little cottage in
Bournemouth waiting for me.

BARWELL. See that's very interesting, because I didn't hear the
word retirement. I heard the words dishonorable discharge.

ABBERLINE. So you've come to rub it in.

BARWELL. I've come to help you.

Fred. We go back a long way. I know things went badly for
you last year and I know that you must be keen to make up
for that.

Why do you think I'm here?

And yes, I want this story on the front pages. Because it's in
the country's interests. But it could be in yours as well.

'Whitechapel Top Cop Busts Aristocratic Sex Scandal'

That has a nice ring to it. One last case. Make the
newspapers, for the right reasons? Hm?

***

Abberline's house.

ABBERLINE *on his knees, praying.*

ABBERLINE. Right so.

Hello. Er. Lord. Father.

Fred Abberline here.

Christ, I don't really know how to

I know we don't talk so much any more, and I'm sorry for
that, I am, but I've been busy you know… and I never really
was one for Sundays. Too much to be done.

Anyway, I wanted to uh… chance my arm and… uh… ask
for mercy. If that's alright.

Look

I know I fucked up. I made mistakes, honest mistakes but

I've worked hard all my life, paid my taxes and done my job.
Upheld the law. Been a faithful husband. And now they're
gonna do me.

Tell me, Lord, should I take this case?

I don't ask you for much.

But I won't
I can't bear to be

Humiliated. Don't let them humiliate me, Lord. Give me that
at least. Give me a chance to redeem myself.

I'd rather be forgotten than remembered like this.

Tell me.
Tell me.
Tell me!

EMILY. Sunrise. And what with no word from the Almighty he
got dressed and headed to St Paul's.

**

The police station. HANKS *is at his desk.*

HANKS. Ohmygawd. You're

They shake hands.

ABBERLINE. Fred Abberline, H Division –

HANKS. I know, sir. Blimey. This is a very big moment for me.

ABBERLINE. Is it?

HANKS. Oh yes, I want you to know, sir, I read everything
about the Ripper case, everything I could get my hands on.

ABBERLINE. Please don't call it that.

HANKS. Took newspaper cuttings, came up with my own
theories, the works

ABBERLINE. Christ, you're one of those.

HANKS. It's the reason why I've applied to be a detective.
I'd love to hear the story some time.

ABBERLINE. Once upon a time there were five women who were killed by a man, it was real and it was fucking horrible the end there you go right I need you to bounce Charlie Swinscow.

HANKS. Oh…
The rent boy?

ABBERLINE. He's an asset in an investigation of mine.

HANKS. Investigation?

If you don't mind, sir –
Are you looking into this place in Fitzrovia?

ABBERLINE. He's mentioned it?

HANKS. He did at first. Seemed to think it would get him off the hook, somehow. He's clammed up, now, of course.

I've got to say,
I've had nothing from Scotland Yard 'bout you looking into it.

ABBERLINE. Right yeah. Well. Strictly speaking, they don't know about it. Yet. And I'd like to keep it that way. Least till I get my bearings.

You'd be doing me a favour, letting him go.

HANKS. I'll be honest, sir, I don't feel comfortable hiding things from the bosses.

But if I were involved in the case, say. Maybe shadowed you, built up some experience…

ABBERLINE. You really wanna be a detective?

***

Emily's kitchen.

ABBERLINE *and* HANKS *have just entered.*

ABBERLINE. Mrs Swinscow I believe we've got something of yours.

CHARLIE *enters.*

CHARLIE. Hi Mum.

She embraces him.

EMILY. He can come home then?

ABBERLINE. We've dropped the charges. On one condition.

Charlie needs to tell us everything about this place he's been working.

HANKS. He won't tell us where it is, won't tell us who runs it.

EMILY. He talks to you, you promise, you keep him out of prison?

ABBERLINE. You got our word on that.

EMILY. What d'you wanna know?

ABBERLINE. Let's start with an address.

EMILY. Charlie? Go on.

CHARLIE. I don't know the address. Fitzrovia somewhere. Got a black door.

ABBERLINE. Alright then. Who got you involved?

CHARLIE. Can't remember.

EMILY. Charlie –

CHARLIE. I can't.

EMILY. It was Henry Newlove.

CHARLIE. Mum!

EMILY. Why you protecting that boy? You think he'd do the same for you?

CHARLIE. Henry ain't to blame.

EMILY. Let them make that decision.
Tell him what he wants to know.

CHARLIE. You'll be nice to him won't you? He won't get in any trouble.

ABBERLINE. Yeah course son. We'll be nice as pie.

***

The interrogation room. NEWLOVE *is being interviewed.*

ABBERLINE. You're a fucking liar!

NEWLOVE. This is persecution!
I should have a solicitor.

ABBERLINE. '*I should have a solicitor.*'

NEWLOVE. If you're gonna ask me questions I should have a fucking solicitor.

ABBERLINE. We've got a witness

NEWLOVE. Charlie Swinscow?

ABBERLINE. Who puts you, Henry Newlove, at the heart of an illicit operation based out of Fitzrovia.

NEWLOVE. An '*illicit operation*'? I'm just a postman.

HANKS. Pull the other one.

NEWLOVE. Think I've delivered to your house, actually. It's the shithole, right?

ABBERLINE. Algernon Allies. George Wright, Ernie Thickbrook. All telegraph boys. Like you.

NEWLOVE. I'm a clerk.

ABBERLINE. And funnily enough, all of them said the same thing as Charlie Swinscow.

HANKS. That they all had the same second job

ABBERLINE. At a place in Fitzrovia.

HANKS. And that second job was given to them by –

ABBERLINE. Henry Newlove.

NEWLOVE. They're lying.

ABBERLINE. Here's how I think it goes. Please feel free to stop me when I get something wrong.

Somehow you get a cushy job in the Telegraph Office.

NEWLOVE. '*Somehow*'?

ABBERLINE. You keep your eye out

NEWLOVE. I got that job on merit.

ABBERLINE. For new lads joining the service.

NEWLOVE. I'm a fucking good postman.

ABBERLINE. Ones who fit a certain. Profile.

Bit naive. Down on their luck.

You pretend to be their best friend, help them get their bearings in their big scary new job, then when the moment's right –

HANKS. You put the moves on them.

ABBERLINE. So when the time comes for you to suggest a bit of extra work on the side –

NEWLOVE. Really imaginative.

HANKS. But if they say no.

ABBERLINE. Well, you've got something over them. The things they've done with you. To you. You threaten to tell their mothers. Their friends. Their boss. And so after that, they work for you.

Is that about the measure of it?

NEWLOVE *pauses. Starts to slow clap.*

NEWLOVE. Detective, that performance was magic, have you been practising?

ABBERLINE. Look, Henry.

NEWLOVE (*to* HANKS). Yours needs a little work, no offence.

ABBERLINE. You're in the muck, mate, sorry to say. We've got enough here to put you away right now. I reckon you're looking at a minimum of two years' hard labour. You ever done hard labour, Henry?

NEWLOVE. Come on

ABBERLINE. What do you think, for Mr Newlove, Constable? The crank or the treadmill.

HANKS. The shot drill I reckon sir, with them arms.

ABBERLINE. Oh yes good idea. You know the shot drill, Henry?

See what they do is, at the crack of dawn they come into your cell and drag you up and out into the prison yard and make you pick up this big rusty cannonball, the kind that scratches all the skin from your arms. And it's heavy, oh yes. Mangles up your back good and proper.

They make you pick it up, walk to the other side of the yard, and then just

Put it down again.

They give you five seconds. Five... four... three... two... one... Then, d'you know what they do?

They make you pick up the cannonball. Walk to the other side of the yard. And put it down. Five... four... three... two –

NEWLOVE. Alright...

ABBERLINE. Two years of doing that and nothing else for fourteen hours a day. What d'you think a young man's body looks like after that?

NEWLOVE. Do I look scared.

ABBERLINE. I don't know, Constable Hanks does he?

HANKS. A bit sir, I'd say.

ABBERLINE. What about when you get out? Gonna be hard to take care of that mother of yours with a mangled back.

NEWLOVE. Why you talking 'bout my mother.

ABBERLINE. Hospitalised for a spell wasn't she?

NEWLOVE. Who told you that

ABBERLINE. Of course Hanks here would do her the courtesy of going up to Camden

NEWLOVE. Don't

ABBERLINE. Letting her know why her son won't be home for supper for a year or two.

NEWLOVE. You don't talk about her. Alright.

You leave that woman be.

ABBERLINE. Give us a name and this all goes away.

NEWLOVE. I tell you what you need and I can go back to work. I have your word?

Beat.

Charles Hammond.

ABBERLINE. Who's that?

NEWLOVE. Thought you was a detective? Hammond used to run one of the busiest molly houses in Soho.

HAMMOND. *There are three key rules to running a place like mine, Henry lad.*

One. Discretion, obviously. Goes without saying.

Two. Comfortable environment. Soft chairs, nice food, polite staff.

And three – and this is the most important one:

Good lighting. I'm serious. No one ever had a nice time somewhere with ugly lighting yunnow what I mean?

End of the day, we're all just animals really aren't we? We're all just little dogs in top hats, you know what I mean, pretending we're one thing when we're really the other, little dogs in top hats, dancing around, getting grumpy when the lights are too bright, getting stroppy when it rains.

This place, my place, it's somewhere people can take off the fucking top hat and have a bit of fun you know. Because isn't that all there is in this miserable world, really, the few fucking seconds where you feel amazing amidst the relentless drudgery of being alive.

And if you can have those few amazing seconds in a place with excellent mood lighting, well then, all the better I say

ABBERLINE. And what were you to him?

NEWLOVE. An employee.

Hammond don't like boys, he likes money.

He was the best in the area. We were always busy. Then you lot changed the law, made it illegal to even look at a fella and all the business dried up.

The clients got spooked, stayed away. Hammond closed up shop. He tells me he's going to America.

HAMMOND. *I wanna see big skies, big skies over flat land and weather oh God I want to see weather and not shit weather like we get here actual weather*

NEWLOVE. And so I think, that's that, you know.

ABBERLINE. So what changed?

NEWLOVE. 'Bout a year later he comes to me and he says.

HAMMOND. *I'm starting a new venture a brand-new business venture*

NEWLOVE. And I tell him he's crackers you know. It's suicide. It'll be six weeks before he's in the cells but he tells me.

HAMMOND. *Nah nah nah it's not gonna be like the old days. It's gonna be a new sort of place. High-end. Drinks, dinner, that sort of thing. I'm taking over a very fine premises in Fitzrovia very fine indeed*

NEWLOVE. And I'm like 'Fitzrovia'? Fuck that, there won't be no clientele. No footfall. But he's like

HAMMOND. *Trust me the clients will come oh yes*

Two years of doing this and we'll never have to work again.

NEWLOVE. So you know, that piqued my curiosity.

HANKS. How's a Soho abbot affording the rent on a place uptown?

NEWLOVE. Well that's just it. He said somebody approached him calling themselves

MR BLACK. *Mr Black.*
  I have a client, Mr Hammond.
  A very special client

HAMMOND. *Nice to be special.*

MR BLACK. *Who has requested your services specifically on
  a new venture. Membership is to be by invitation only. My
  client and a select group of other individuals.*

HAMMOND. *I'm retired.*

MR BLACK. *If you can guarantee privacy and discretion, they
  are willing to pay a very good price.*

HAMMOND. *It don't matter how much they pay, my friend, the
  clients won't come if they think the police'll be at our door
  every five minutes*

MR BLACK. *The police will not interfere. They've been
  informed and instructed that this particular premises is
  off-limits to any sort of arrest.*

ABBERLINE. Say that again.

NEWLOVE. Immunity. Hammond told me we'd never get our
  door kicked in again. There was a deal, like I said.

  I see that was horseshit, of course.

  A moment. ABBERLINE *takes this in.*

ABBERLINE. Any officers ever come to this place?

NEWLOVE. Not in uniform.

HANKS. And what was your role in all this?

HAMMOND. *You're gonna be my new recruiter.*

  *I'm gonna need new boys for this, none of the old crowd
  will do.*

NEWLOVE. *You know, they're looking for people at the
  General Post Office.*

HAMMOND. *So what?*

NEWLOVE. *So telegraph boys, they don't pay them nothing.*

It was easy really. Every boy that worked out, I'd get a cut of their earnings.

ABBERLINE. Where's the house?

NEWLOVE. Told you enough.

HANKS. We'll see if the magistrate agrees.

NEWLOVE *pauses. Reconsiders.*

NEWLOVE. Number Nineteen

Cleveland Street.

***

A pub, later. HANKS *brings over some drinks.*

HANKS. I'm not gonna lie to you sir.
I'm excited. I really am.

This is a very big moment for me. An actual raid. Tonight. I'm gonna be a part of it. Will we kick down the door?

ABBERLINE. That's the idea.

HANKS. I'm very excited.
Can I ask, which one of us gets to kick it? Because I don't mind but I've never done it before, is there like a technique or –

ABBERLINE. We've still got a couple of hours. You should eat something.

HANKS. I couldn't eat a thing sir, I'm sure of it. I keep wondering if they'll draw me in the newspaper.
I was wondering.
What about the deputy?
The commissioner? Shouldn't we let them know that we're pushing ahead with the investigation.

ABBERLINE. Eat something, Hanks. It's gonna be a long night.

***

EMILY*'s kitchen. She goes to check on the stew.*

She tastes it.

Seasons it. Tastes it again.

EMILY. When told she was carrying a child, Emily had been barely more'n a child herself.

Her father had passed two months prior, she was sharing a small room with her mother and two noisy strangers and the dalliance with the landlord's son Thomas had been her only bit of sunshine.

And what sunshine!

But then of course she started to show and
After a shotgun marriage to a baby-faced Tom
She spent her every waking moment,
Wishing the child away.
Asking her God
To please give her a few more years of girlhood.

But then the birth arrived
And the child was born
Still and grey.

And silent.

And suddenly she felt shamed to ever have thought it.

God forgive her.

But then. Like that.

The sound of a baby crying.

He cried. Ha!

He cried! A miracle. Heaven's angels singing.

He was just being quiet. Biding his time 'fore he said hello to the world.

Charlie.

***

The private dining room.

SOMERSET. With William.

EUSTON. Yes?

SOMERSET. Was there. Has there ever been any. Confusion. A moment where, say one of you said or expressed something and the other was a little reticent.

EUSTON. Not that I can –

SOMERSET. They're not returning my letters.

EUSTON. You're talking about –

SOMERSET. My thunderbolt.

EUSTON. Ah. How many letters have you sent

SOMERSET. One or two.

Five.

EUSTON. Five

SOMERSET. Is that too many?

EUSTON. With no response?

SOMERSET. That is too many.

EUSTON. They're probably just busy.

SOMERSET. Or maybe I should send another letter.

EUSTON. I wouldn't do that.

SOMERSET. Just a short one explaining –

EUSTON. I really wouldn't. Look if you're really worried. Just talk to them.

SOMERSET. Talk?

EUSTON. Go and be honest and tell them how you feel and say if they don't feel the same way then they need to tell you

SOMERSET. As easy as that.
Yes. Yes alright. I'll go and see them.

***

Number 19 Cleveland Street.

Later that night. A loud knocking. We hear a voice from the street outside.

HANKS (*offstage*). Charles Hammond!

This is the Metropolitan Police open up!

Knock knock knock.

Open up or we'll kick down the door!

Knock knock knock.

We're giving you to the count of five!

One… two… three… four –

ABBERLINE *walks straight in.*

ABBERLINE. Door was open.

Inside Cleveland Street.

ABBERLINE *stands in an empty house.*

EMILY. Inside Nineteen Cleveland Street, the detective noticed two things. The first was that the lighting was exceptionally well thought-out. The second was that there was no one there.

ABBERLINE. Deserted. Jesus.

We're too fucking late.

HANKS *enters.*

HANKS. Looks like it's been empty for a couple of days.

ABBERLINE. Newlove must've known they'd already scarpered when he tipped us off.

HANKS. No sign of Hammond.

There's a knock at the door.

ABBERLINE. See who that is, will you?

HANKS *opens the door. It's* SOMERSET.

HANKS. Hello?

SOMERSET. Who are you?

HANKS. I'm Constable Hanks mate, who are you?

SOMERSET. Constable? You're a policeman.

HANKS. Were you looking for someone, Mr –

SOMERSET. Brown. Mr Brown. That's right that's me.

No. I.

Actually. I. I think I've got the wrong door. Yes.

Actually yes looking at it oh this door is a totally different door to the door I was hoping to knock on.

You have a nice day Constable.

The man leaves. ABBERLINE *watches him go.*

ABBERLINE. I know that man. I'm sure.
That's Lord Arthur Somerset.

HANKS. Right yeah.

Who's that then?

***

Knightsbridge Barracks.

The private quarters of Lord Arthur George Somerset.

ABBERLINE. Interview conducted on 22nd July, 1889 by Detective Inspector Frederick Abberline, in the presence of Police Constable Hanks who will also be taking notes.

Could you state your name for the record, sir.

SOMERSET. Really?

He sighs.

Lord Arthur George Somerset

ABBERLINE. And you reside at Knightsbridge Barracks is that correct?

SOMERSET. You're in my quarters. You're literally sitting by my bed.

Yes that's / where I live

ABBERLINE. Thank you very much for helping us with our enquiries Lord Somerset

SOMERSET. Fine.

ABBERLINE. We'll try to be quick as we can.

Yesterday afternoon you knocked on the door of a Number Nineteen Cleveland Street.

SOMERSET. If you say so.

ABBERLINE. Can I ask what you were doing there?

SOMERSET. As I told the officer at the time.
I was mistaken. I knocked on –

ABBERLINE. The wrong door.

SOMERSET. Yes.

ABBERLINE. Perfectly understandable.

HANKS. We've all been there!

ABBERLINE. Funny thing is that door you accidentally knocked on

HANKS. Number Nineteen, Cleveland Street

ABBERLINE. Has for some time now been operating as a brothel.

SOMERSET. Goodness. Has it really?
That is surprising. In Fitzrovia?

HANKS. Area's going to hell.

ABBERLINE. So when one of my officers catches someone like yourself, knocking on a door like that well, it's only right we start to wonder what you were doing there.

SOMERSET. Like I said. I –

ABBERLINE. Got the wrong door.

SOMERSET. I was looking for a friend's house. Samuel Robeson.

I'm often uh visiting Mr Robeson in my capacity as Equerry to His Highness the Prince of Wales.

I'm in charge of purchasing, racing and breeding His
Highness's horses. He's going to be very concerned if I'm
away from my duties for too long today so if you don't mind –

ABBERLINE. Well perhaps we can get a message to His
Highness then, tell him you're helping us with our enquiries.

Beat.

SOMERSET. I'm sure that won't be necessary. Just let's. Get
this over with.

HANKS *passes* SOMERSET *a folder.*

ABBERLINE. If you could take a look at this, sir.

SOMERSET. Yes?

ABBERLINE. This is a banker's draft for the amount of fifteen
pounds. It was found in the bureau of an office upstairs in
Number Nineteen Cleveland Street. The bureau belongs to
a Mr Charles Hammond, whereabouts currently unknown.
The banker's draft is also addressed to Mr Hammond. Do
you recognise the signature at the bottom?

SOMERSET *nods.*

SOMERSET. Okay so

So. I'll tell you what happened.
I'll I'll tell you exactly.

So. Yes. I was in the area, I'd been for a short jolly around
the park and a woman, a comely woman mind, well dressed
not a street walker, she came up to me and handed me a card
for a 'tableu plastique' you know

And well. I thought. I'm a man dammit I'm a single man and
I thought to myself Arthur if you want to go and watch nice-
looking women in a state of undress then that's your
prerogative. But of course once I got inside and I found out
what sort of establishment well I turned tail so fast –

ABBERLINE. So you're saying you went inside. Left straight
away.

SOMERSET. Oh yes.

ABBERLINE. And the banker's draft?

SOMERSET. I must have bought a drink.

ABBERLINE. An expensive drink, fifteen pounds?

SOMERSET. I remember thinking that at the time.

ABBERLINE. Constable Hanks, if you would pass Lord
Somerset the second file.

He does.

We also found this letter locked in Mr Hammond's bureau.

A letter addressed to one of the Cleveland Street boys. You
probably don't know any of the Cleveland Street boys, do
you? George Wright, Ernie Thickbrook, Charlie Swinscow?

SOMERSET. No

ABBERLINE. What about a boy called –

HANKS. Algernon Allies.

ABBERLINE. Do you know young Mr Allies, Arthur?

SOMERSET. I. No.

ABBERLINE. Is that your handwriting?

SOMERSET. No.

ABBERLINE. Looks a lot like the one on the banker's draft.
What about the signature. What does it say Hanks?

HANKS. Think it says 'Podge' sir.

ABBERLINE. Podge.

Beat.

Do you recognise that name? Podge?

SOMERSET. Why would I?

ABBERLINE. No one ever called you that? Not a little
nickname, a term of affection

HANKS. Quite sweet really, isn't it. 'Podge'

ABBERLINE. 'Podge'

SOMERSET. No. I'm sorry. Never. The letter isn't mine. If that's all you've got then –

ABBERLINE. D'you know I'm gasping.
Why don't we take a break.

Think we could all use a drink.

I'll nip down to the mess and do us a pot of tea. Fancy a tea Constable Hanks?

HANKS. I wouldn't say no, sir.

ABBERLINE. Anything for you, Podge?

SOMERSET. No thank you.

A moment. He realises. ABBERLINE *grins.*

I mean.

Now I

I only responded because you said

That doesn't mean

ABBERLINE. Do you know what's in this letter Lord Somerset?

SOMERSET. Why would I.

HANKS. Shall I read it out loud?

SOMERSET. I don't think that's

ABBERLINE. If you'd be so kind Constable –

HANKS. 'Dear Algernon, since we last met on Tuesday week, my thoughts have turned to nothing else'

SOMERSET. Okay listen

HANKS. '– but the touch of your skin on mine, the thought of your hands running through my – '

SOMERSET. Alright! There's.

There's no need.

Christ. Is nothing private in this world.

I

I need a drink. Can I have a drink?

ABBERLINE *nods.* HANKS *pours* SOMERSET *a Scotch.*

ABBERLINE. Why don't you start again from the beginning?

ARTHUR SOMERSET *takes a deep breath. He nods.*

SOMERSET. I can't remember who first told me about it.

This place that was perfectly safe.

Completely discreet. Where for once, the police would leave
you alone. You'd don't understand what it's been like these
past few years, since Labouchère –

ABBERLINE. So it's our fault.

SOMERSET. I didn't say that.

But when I got there, it surpassed my expectations.

This was a nice place to be, you understand. Not seedy.
Welcoming. A place a gentleman could be comfortable.

It was my third or fourth visit when I met

Algie.

HANKS. This is Algernon Allies?

SOMERSET. Yes. He was like something from a painting.

We went upstairs of course but when we got there. We didn't
do anything. We conversed. He asked me a question. I asked
him a question. We talked about our lives and the world, our
families

One of those conversations where before you realise it it's
morning.

After that we became. Friends. More than that.

We enjoyed each other.

ABBERLINE. He told you that did he?

SOMERSET. Well, yes actually –

ABBERLINE. You think any of those boys would be in that room if they didn't have to be?

SOMERSET. Now listen, we were two people, two human beings and actually I think that's, that's very presumptuous of you

ABBERLINE. *'Presumptuous'*?

SOMERSET. He can make his own decisions and

And actually if you ask him I think you'll find –

Suddenly ABBERLINE *loses it, knocks the drink out of* SOMERSET*'s hand.*

ABBERLINE. Shut the fuck up! Alright? Just shut up.
Now
We wanna know who's behind this operation.
We wanna know how they infiltrated the Telegraph Service.
We wanna know who's bankrolling it.

SOMERSET. I don't know any of those things!

ABBERLINE. Liar.

HANKS. Sir

ABBERLINE. Fucking liar.

SOMERSET. I don't!

HANKS puts a hand on ABBERLINE*'s shoulder.*

HANKS. Let's take it easy, eh?

ABBERLINE lets him go. He dusts himself off. Pours himself a Scotch.

ABBERLINE. Lord Arthur George Somerset. I'm placing you under arrest on suspicion of gross indecency –

SOMERSET. No.

ABBERLINE. Stand up and face the wall –

SOMERSET. No wait. You can't. This will ruin me. I can give you names. Anything you need. Hammond. Ch-Charles Hammond. He runs the place.

HANKS. We know that already.

SOMERSET. Then then okay alright I can. There's more. Please. There's a lot more.

I have information. Information your superiors won't want me repeating.

ABBERLINE. And what's that?

SOMERSET. Not here. I can't say here.

I want a lawyer. Let me talk to a lawyer and get some guarantees.

Give me a week, and then I'll sit down and I'll tell you everything.

ABBERLINE. Two days. And if you're not here when we come back, these letters are going straight to *The Times*.

***

The Hand and Marigold pub. Knightsbridge.

ABBERLINE. I shouldn't have lost my temper.

HANKS. I'll be honest sir.

I thought I'd be more excited. Arthur Somerset. That's who we're chasing is it? Did you see his face at the end, he's terrified.

ABBERLINE. Ah, fuck him. Without punters, this place don't exist. He's as guilty as anyone.

HANKS. I was thinking, with this Somerset lead, maybe it's time to take this to the bosses.

ABBERLINE. No! Not yet. Not until we've found Hammond. Whatever Somerset does or doesn't give us, Hammond's the only one who can corroborate. He's the one getting paid, he's the one who knows.

I've got to find Hammond before the commissioner finds out what we're doing and takes me off the case.

HANKS. Why would he do that?

ABBERLINE. You ain't heard?

Next week Moore is gonna publish his report into
Whitechapel. It'll be plastered all over every newspaper in
the country. And you know what it's gonna say?

Frederick Abberline: the man who let the killer go.

HANKS. Let him go?

ABBERLINE. Three weeks before the first Whitechapel murder.

These girls who worked in the laundry came to me at the
station and said that this bloke they knew, this... neighbour.
He'd been saying things... threatening women... spooking
people and would I look into it.

And so I went, and I spoke to the fella. And there didn't
seem anything odd about him. And so I left it alone.

And then Polly Nichols got killed.

And the laundry girls came back, and they said, everyone
knows it was him what did it. The same fella I spoke to.

HANKS. Jesus. And what did you do?

ABBERLINE. Well I noted it down, but. It was just talk. And
with the circus around the case –

I never got round to following it up.
Anyway, the two girls left the city, frightened.
By the time they got back, five women were dead and this
neighbour of theirs had jumped off Southwark Bridge.

HANKS. It was him?

ABBERLINE. Who the hell knows. But when Moore took over
the case, the same girls came to him and told them how
I hadn't listened, and now they're going public with it and
I look like a fucking joke.

HANKS. I gotta ask. Why didn't you follow up?

ABBERLINE. Ach, this neighbour of theirs, he didn't fit the
profile. We had a profile of who we were looking for and he
wasn't it. He was just

Some bloke.

And these girls were ranting and raving, half-cut. Sort of women who might do something like that just to get in the papers, you know?

HANKS. I know sir, but even so –

ABBERLINE. Any detective woulda done the same and now they're gonna do me for it, they'll do me and for the rest of time I'll be the man who lost Jack the Ripper God I hate that fucking stupid name

I got no kids. This is my legacy.

But if we can bring this Cleveland Street thing in

Debrief Somerset. Find Hammond. See if he corroborates. Hammond's still the key.

We find him and we've got a case.

***

Emily's kitchen. EMILY *admires her plate.*

EMILY. Emily couldn't remember the first time she'd heard the story told by every Willow pattern plate.

Her mother maybe, some dinner long ago.

The story of a princess who fell in love with a low-born poet

The poet worked day and night as a servant for the princess's father, the king, which meant that whenever he got home he was too knackered to write any poetry.

Now, the king didn't like the idea of his little girl and this low-born bloke, so he sent his men to arrest the poet but before he could

The couple ran. They ran far away to a little island somewhere and they built a little blue house.

BARWELL *talks to* CHARLIE.

BARWELL. I wanted to ask you a favour, Charlie. A friend of mine, Mr Parke, is a journalist for the *North London Press*. He would like to talk to you about this house in Cleveland Street.

CHARLIE. Why would I do that?

BARWELL. A story in the paper would build public support, help speed the investigation along, help you get back to work. You would be anonymous, your name will be nowhere near it. What do you say?

EMILY. In the little blue house the couple were happy. They were so happy that at the end of the day the poet had so much energy that he could write and write and write and soon enough he was writing enough to make a living.

BARWELL. I want you both to know you can knock on my door any time. You're not alone in this.

He leaves.

EMILY. The more he wrote the more his reputation grew, until he became so famous that news of this brilliant writer got back to the king, who put two and two together and sent his soldiers to the island where they kicked down the door.

ABBERLINE *is in their kitchen.*

ABBERLINE. No more messing about. I need to find Charles Hammond.

CHARLIE. I don't know where he is!

EMILY. When the soldiers found the couple, they stabbed the poet through the heart and set fire to the little blue house with the princess inside. Killing them both.

ABBERLINE. Now listen to me you little shit. We dropped your charges on the condition you helped our case and as of this moment you've given us fuck all so if you really wanna stay out of prison I'd come up with something fast.

EMILY. Which is when the gods, feeling bad for the poor dead couple, took their spirits and reincarnated them as two birds, so they could always be together.

Which is nice.

***

SOMERSET. Say something.

Say something Fitz please. I can't sit in silence with you
emanating all this

Judgement.

EUSTON. Judgement? You're a bloody fool Arthur

What were you thinking
Going to a place like that.

SOMERSET. It's alright for you and your William and his
obliging mother but for the rest of us out here

We have to take our chances.

How bad do you think it is?

EUSTON. Bad. They have these letters?

SOMERSET. Yes.

EUSTON. Your signature?

SOMERSET. Oh my God. Hammond must have kept the letters!

Of course! I addressed the letters I wrote to Algernon to
Cleveland Street and they found them in Hammond's bureau,
so Algie must never have got them! So don't you see, Fitz, it
wasn't that he was ignoring me, he never got the chance to
read them! Oh I'm so relieved.

EUSTON. Listen to yourself. You should be behind bars and
this is what you're worried about?

SOMERSET. I know it sounds / mad but

EUSTON. Podge

SOMERSET. We had a real

EUSTON. Don't say it

SOMERSET. Connection. We do.

EUSTON. Arthur. You were paying him.

SOMERSET. I know but that doesn't mean –

EUSTON. But hang on
If they have all of this evidence why aren't you locked up?

SOMERSET. Ah. Well. I panicked. I threatened them

EUSTON. With what.

SOMERSET. I have a trump card. Sensitive information.

EUSTON. What information?

SOMERSET. A name. Someone I saw at Cleveland Street.

EUSTON. What name?

SOMERSET. I can't.

I really can't.

If I tell you. You have to swear to keep it to yourself –

Swear it!

EUSTON. Alright. I swear.

SOMERSET. Every time I was there I saw

Prince Eddy.

Pause. EUSTON *takes this in.*

EUSTON. Prince Eddy. The Queen's grandson?

SOMERSET. That's right.

EUSTON. In a house full of telegraph boys.

SOMERSET. Oh yes.

EUSTON. Well. Fuck.

SOMERSET. I know.

EUSTON. Fuck!

SOMERSET. I came downstairs and there he was. He said hello and he looked surprised to see me and he had that look of his. Those eyes. That strange smile.

I was terrified, obviously. I mean I work for his father. But Eddy was calm.

Asked about my mother, finished his drink and he went upstairs. Like it was nothing.

He was very at home.

So you see. If that doesn't make them drop the investigation then I don't know what will.

EUSTON. You told this to the police?

SOMERSET. Not yet but

EUSTON. You can't seriously be considering using this?

SOMERSET. What other choice do I have?

EUSTON. You're going to tell the police that the future king was frequenting a Fitzrovia brothel. They'll ruin you Arthur.

What about your position? You work for his father.

SOMERSET. The Prince of Wales? He won't find out. He won't find out.

EUSTON. Of course he'll find out! As soon as you say anything to the police the whole world will know –

SOMERSET. Well what am I supposed to do then! Tell me, Fitz because I've got to do something!

Pause.

What if. What if you helped me? Your godfather.

EUSTON. What about him?

SOMERSET. He loves you and he would do anything for you and he also happens to be

EUSTON. The Home Secretary.

SOMERSET. You go to him and you say, you don't mention my name, but you've heard rumours, about, about the prince and the brothel, but you don't mention my name, you go to him and you say that two nosy police officers have been sniffing around and if they're not careful they'll expose all manner of trouble, because there are people, there are people willing to talk, but you don't mention my name at all

EUSTON. If he asks –

SOMERSET. And you say you don't know specifics. Please Fitz. I'm begging you. You're my only hope in this.

EMILY. And because he was a loyal friend

And a good friend

EUSTON. Alright

EMILY. Lord Euston went to his godfather and he said what he had to

SOMERSET. Thank you, Fitz. I mean it.

EMILY. And didn't use Somerset's name and his godfather patted him on the shoulder and said something like

HOME SECRETARY. Well my lad, thanks for bringing this to me discreetly.

EMILY. And that was that and all seemed well and maybe it would have been fine except that very soon afterwards a telegram arrived stating that

BERTIE. His Royal Highness the Prince of Wales

BERTIE, *Prince of Wales, appears in shadow.*

EMILY. Bertie, to his friends

BERTIE. Would cordially like to invite Henry Fitzroy, Earl of Euston for lunch

EUSTON. Ohhh

F–

Blackout.

ACT TWO

A palace dining hall. BERTIE *and* EUSTON *are eating dinner.*

BERTIE. You seem nervous Fitz.

EUSTON. Sir?

BERTIE. Have a little more wine.

EUSTON *pours himself a little.*

Good bottle that. Old Lord Sefton gave it to me. Of course that was before he found out I'd been tupping his wife.

You ever meet Lady Sefton? Gorgeous woman. Wonderfully fat. Knows what to do with a fellow if you know what I mean.

EUSTON. Yes sir.

BERTIE. Do you know what I mean, Fitz?

EUSTON. I –

BERTIE. You're an unmarried man, man about town –

EUSTON. Yes.

BERTIE. Get stuck into a nice little filly every once in a while?

EUSTON. Right.

Silence. They eat their meals.

I wondered, sir. About this invitation. I was honoured to be asked. And so last-minute –

BERTIE. Well isn't that kind.

EUSTON. But I'm still.

BERTIE. Yes?

EUSTON. Wondering. What exactly it is. I've been summoned for.

BERTIE. Summoned!

EUSTON. Yes.

BERTIE. What a dramatic word. We're having a friendly chat over dinner! How's your veal?

EUSTON. Oh it's –

BERTIE. I fucking love veal if I could eat it morning noon and dinner I would. There is this little place in Paris and the way that they do it, one mouthful and I am transported to Elysium.

I've tried to get the chefs here to replicate it but it's like asking a blind dog to play the cello.

EUSTON. Well I think. This is very nice.

BERTIE (*shouts*). You there! Bring us more wine!

I'd like to talk to you about my son.

EUSTON. Prince Eddy?

BERTIE. Do you and he ever cross paths?

EUSTON. Occasionally.

BERTIE. At parties.

EUSTON. Yes.

BERTIE. Gatherings

EUSTON. Sure.

BERTIE. Anywhere else?

EUSTON. I –

BERTIE. What does he get up to? What are his interests?

EUSTON. You'd know better than I would, sir.

BERTIE. He can be quite misunderstood, poor thing. I made a promise to his mother to keep him out of trouble and I'm doing my very best but –

Do you know, people keep spreading the strangest rumours about him.

EUSTON. Really sir? That's awful.

BERTIE. Isn't it!

Funny thing rumours. Lord knows how they spread.

I heard one about you, the other day actually.

EUSTON. Can't have been that interesting.

BERTIE. Something about a gentlemen friend who you've grown rather close to. Little trysts up at his mother's house.

EUSTON *freezes*.

Relax, man, you look like you've seen a ghost. A birdy told a birdy told me and I thought to myself well I'm glad he's having fun! That's all.

I'm glad he's having fun but wouldn't it be a shame if such a promising young man jeopardised his

future.

You know? Because if the wrong people found out –

EUSTON. Sir –

Beat.

BERTIE. I had a very interesting telegram from the Home Secretary yesterday morning. He speaks very highly of you. Loves his godson. Wants to see him on the right path.

He told me you came to see him and told him that some mysterious figure is threatening to spread the most awful lies about Prince Eddy –

EUSTON. I... I can explain.

BERTIE. Yes I bet you can.

EUSTON. I don't. I think my godfather was mis–

BERTIE. Who's spreading the rumours?

EUSTON. I don't know. I can't tell you. I'm sorry, sir.

BERTIE. This lover of yours. What's his name?

EUSTON. I. That isn't –

BERTIE. William, isn't it?

Works for my brother, so I hear.

Perhaps I should put in a word. Save you from yourself.

Yes, William might be the sort of chap who might benefit from a posting abroad. India perhaps. What do you say to that?

EUSTON (*softly*). Please.

BERTIE. I didn't hear you?

EUSTON. Please don't send him away.

BERTIE. I love my son. Deeply and truly.

And he'll be king one day.

All of which is to say, we will go to a great many lengths to protect him.

Now.

I'm going to ask you again.

Have you heard any rumours about my son?

EUSTON. Y-yes.

BERTIE. That he's been seen at a brothel in Fitzrovia.

EUSTON. Yes.

BERTIE. And who's been spreading these rumours?

EUSTON. I can't, sir.

BERTIE. Yes you can.

EUSTON. Arthur.

It's Arthur Somerset.

BERTIE. Pity.

***

EMILY. Of all the conversations that altered the future of Charlie and Emily Swinscow, there are plenty more we could spend time worrying about.

But one mattered more than most. The one that started with a telegram that said

BERTIE *gets a telegram.*

And suddenly QUEEN VICTORIA *arrives in all her splendour.*

VICTORIA. Her Majesty Victoria, Queen of Great Britain and Ireland,
Would cordially like to invite her son, Bertie, Prince of Wales for tea.

BERTIE. Oh Christ.

***

Buckingham Palace.

Dining room.

The sound of cutlery on crockery. Scrape scrape scrape.

BERTIE. Well, I must say

VICTORIA. I'm hot.

BERTIE. This is nice.

VICTORIA. I'm sweating.

BERTIE. Spending time together.

VICTORIA. Smell me I'm sweating.

BERTIE. Mother and son.

VICTORIA. Open a window.

BERTIE. It's freezing outside.

VICTORIA. What is this it's disgusting.

BERTIE. It's pickled herring.

VICTORIA. Why is it pickled?

BERTIE. Because it's pickled herring.

VICTORIA. It looks like someone sneezed.

BERTIE. Do you want something else?

VICTORIA. Of course I want something else I can't live off air alone I'm not a cactus.

BERTIE. How's the garden coming along?

VICTORIA. I don't want to talk about that.

BERTIE. Well, how are things going with Lord Salisbury?

VICTORIA. I don't want to talk about that either.

You are always so nosy, Bertie, always burying your snout into other people's business like a big fat truffling hog.

BERTIE. Well. Like I said. This is nice.

The sound of cutlery on crockery.

Alix sends her love.

VICTORIA. Still boring is she?

BERTIE. And the boys. Eddy and George. They're both well.

VICTORIA. Are they.

BERTIE. George is enjoying his new posting.

VICTORIA. And Eddy. No issues?

BERTIE. No.

VICTORIA. No problems?

No nasty rumours floating around?

BERTIE. I don't know what exactly –

VICTORIA. Are they true?

BERTIE. No of course not.

Look Mama, whatever you might have heard about Eddy, I don't want you to worry.

VICTORIA. I do worry.

BERTIE. Because I'm taking care of it.

VICTORIA. That's what worries me.

BERTIE. Plans are in motion.

VICTORIA. Plans

BERTIE. Measures are being taken. To make sure that this gets
no further.

VICTORIA. But if they are only rumours

BERTIE. Yes –

VICTORIA. And not true. Then why do anything at all?

BERTIE. I don't –

VICTORIA. I mean people say awful things about you all the
time –

BERTIE. Do they?

VICTORIA. The most horrible things and we don't pay any
heed to it. I say maintain a dignified silence.

BERTIE. Yes. Well that's one way to approach it but

VICTORIA. Put our fingers in our ears / and say la la la la la

BERTIE. But of course an alternative plan of action would be to
stop these rumours getting out of hand to save there being
any sort of stain on Eddy's reputation.

This man. Arthur Somerset. He works for me. Which means
there are things we can do to ensure that he keeps schtum.

VICTORIA. Things you can do?

BERTIE. That's right.

VICTORIA. Let the man alone Bertie.

BERTIE. Mama –

VICTORIA. He can't prove anything?

BERTIE. Of course not.

VICTORIA. So let him alone.

BERTIE. Except maybe

VICTORIA. Except?

BERTIE. Maybe he can. Perhaps. There might be. An ounce. Of truth. A smidgen

VICTORIA. To which part.

BERTIE. A few of the different constituent parts but I don't know for certain

VICTORIA. This brothel?

BERTIE. Yes.

VICTORIA. And the boys

BERTIE. Perhaps

VICTORIA. So when you said the rumours weren't true

BERTIE. Mm.

VICTORIA. What you meant was

BERTIE. They are. In fact. True. Yes.
I say, this marmalade is rather nice.

VICTORIA. You spoiled that boy you know.

His mother insisted on breastfeeding him herself. I said at the time, women are not cows. But of course nobody listens to me. I've only had about a hundred children.

BERTIE. You know we have to do something to protect his / reputation

VICTORIA. I don't know that

BERTIE. Mama –

VICTORIA. I don't know that. I don't see that we have to do anything actually because if your son has been foolish enough to behave like this –

BERTIE. It's just high spirits

VICTORIA. To break the law

BERTIE. Rambunctiousness

VICTORIA. the law of this land then let him deal with the consequences.

BERTIE. Very funny. Yes.

VICTORIA. I'm not laughing.

The scrape of cutlery on crockery.

BERTIE. Mummy.

Mummy, come now.

This is no joke. The consequences here would mean.
Disgrace. Arrest, even. Prison. Think of the press. If Eddy is
arrested then the scandal it would cause –

VICTORIA. I worry. Bertie. About what awaits me in the beyond.

I am afraid that when the time comes I will be damned.

BERTIE. Listen, Mama.

Please.

I hear what you're saying.

But I really think you're worrying over nothing.

No one's facing damnation. Not for a silly thing like this.

Eddy's just letting off steam. That's all. If you just let me
take care of it –

VICTORIA. No. I'm sorry Bertie, I can't allow it.

BERTIE. You'll destroy his life.

VICTORIA. He should have thought of that.

BERTIE. Don't you have any feeling for your grandson?

Alright then.

Alright.

What about me

VICTORIA. What about *you*?

BERTIE. There's a worry.

A slight worry that if the police start looking too closely at
this Cleveland Street business

If they follow the money

That they might find some suggestion

That I might have

May have

Had some small part to play in setting it up.

Beat.

VICTORIA. Where's the mustard

There are sausages on my plate and I always have mustard on my sausages.

BERTIE. Look I didn't mean

Someone came to me and said wouldn't it be good if Eddy always had somewhere safe and private to go.

Where the law couldn't

Where he wouldn't be

And I thought that sounded like an excellent idea so I said

I told them to go ahead and

All I was doing was trying to protect him. Protect the family. That's all.

Well. Say something will you.

Pause.

VICTORIA. Bertie.

I don't say this lightly.

But sometimes I wonder whether in all the world there is a mother who is more continually disappointed in her child than I am in you.

Do you know. The moment you were born and they first handed you to me. Everyone told me how I would be overwhelmed by emotion and connection and love.

About how the moment that the doctor passed you to me

I would feel

The presence of God.

And in the months I was carrying you I looked forward to that moment every day.

But when it came

When you wriggled out of me and they passed you over I couldn't feel anything. I looked at you I looked at your fat little face and I couldn't feel anything.

And in all the years since I have waited for that feeling to come, and every time you walk through the door I think maybe this will be the day maybe this will be the day I feel it,

and then I look up at your face and it's just the same old disappointment.

BERTIE. You think I need your approval?

VICTORIA. I refuse to be damned, Bertie.

BERTIE. Well then you better start praying for salvation.

***

Knightsbridge Barracks.

The stables.

EUSTON. You've done a wonderful job with these stables, Arthur. That piebald really is beautiful.

SOMERSET. He was a cast-off from Lord Matthews if you can believe it?
Bit of a lost soul.

EUSTON. Well perhaps you'll have a chance to add another to the collection.

I've

I've been entrusted to pass this along.

SOMERSET. What's this?

EUSTON. It's something that I think will solve a lot of problems.

SOMERSET *opens the envelope he's just been handed.*

SOMERSET. A ticket to France? Fitz, what's going on?

EUSTON. The Prince of Wales has requested that you attend a horse fair on his behalf. In Avignon.

SOMERSET. There's no horse fair in Avignon.

EUSTON. It's new, apparently.

SOMERSET *looks at the ticket.*

SOMERSET. Wait, why would His Highness give you this? Why would he give it to you and not me?

EUSTON. He knew that I would be seeing you.

SOMERSET. That doesn't make sense –

EUSTON. Arthur.

SOMERSET. Wait.

No.

EUSTON. Now listen

SOMERSET. He knows?

No no no

How would he –

Unless.

You told him.
Oh Fitz, why?

EUSTON. I didn't have a choice. They know about –

SOMERSET. William.

EUSTON. I'm so sorry. I really am –

But

This won't go away, Podge. You realise that. These boys have already started talking to the newspapers. How long till people put two and two together?

The police could be back at your door at any moment and
when they are it is better for everyone that you are safely out
of the country on royal business at the horse fair in Avignon

SOMERSET. THERE IS NO HORSE FAIR IN AVIGNON!

EUSTON. Arthur –

SOMERSET. Don't

I said don't touch me.

I need – I need a moment –

SOMERSET *breaks off*. EUSTON *lets him go*.

***

VICTORIA. Almighty God radiant with light.

Your faithful servant Victoria Regina begs you for guidance

And lays before you all that weighs heavy on my heart.

Can you hear me, Lord?

Tell me what to do about my grandson.

Tell me what I should do to save my soul.

Tell me
Tell me

Tell me!

And then suddenly

Sunlight! Glorious music!

Time stops as

God Almighty

*Or, at least, Victoria's version of God, appears in her
bedroom.*

And They say –

GOD. HELLO VICTORIA.

VICTORIA. My… Lord God?

GOD. GUILTY, AS CHARGED.

VICTORIA. You heard my prayer?

GOD. I HEAR YOU WHEN YOU SAY YOUR PRAYERS
I HEAR YOU WHEN YOU SING IN THE BATH I HEARD
YOU WHEN YOU USED TO WHISPER IN YOUR
HUSBAND'S EAR IN THE MIDDLE OF THE NIGHT.

VICTORIA. I had no idea.

Things are being done in my name.

My grandson faces scandal and ruin and my people will do
whatever it takes to protect him.

GOD. AND YOU WANT TO STOP THEM?

VICTORIA. Yes.

GOD. WHY?

VICTORIA. Because it is the right thing to do.

GOD. I DON'T BELIEVE YOU.

VICTORIA. Because we are not above the law.

GOD. TRY AGAIN.

VICTORIA. Because I am afraid.

GOD. BETTER.

VICTORIA. I am so afraid, Lord. I have spent my life listening
to people like my son say things like

'We'll take care of it'
and
'We'll make it go away'

And of course I know what they really mean
But I smile
And I nod
And I don't ask any questions. And another sin gets tallied to
my name.

And now I'm afraid that when the time comes I will face
fiery damnation.

Show me what to do, Lord. Please. Show me the path to salvation.

GOD. COME CHILD. TELL ME EVERYTHING.

***

A rooftop, high above the city. NEWLOVE *and* CHARLIE *share a cigarette.*

NEWLOVE. How'd you find me?

CHARLIE. You brought me up here once. You remember. They went looking for you at the Post Office.

NEWLOVE. Unfortunately I've had to part ways with our former employer. Arseholes. Something about two coppers carting me off the mail-room floor.

CHARLIE. I didn't plan any of this.

NEWLOVE. You're a fuckin grass.

CHARLIE. They were gonna do me for thieving. You told me it was fine! You told me police knew about it –

NEWLOVE. That's what Hammond told me.

CHARLIE. Where is Hammond, Henry?

NEWLOVE. How should I know?

CHARLIE. Why you protecting him? Case you haven't noticed he's fucked off and it's me and you that are left and if they don't find him who d'you think they're gonna come for?

NEWLOVE. I really liked that job, you know. At the Post Office. I only got it so I could find boys for Hammond but once I got there.

You reckon there's a world where I coulda been a postman and just a postman. Like.

Normal job normal house normal everything. You think there's a world where that happens.

CHARLIE. Yeah. I do.

NEWLOVE. Well. It ain't this one.

NEWLOVE *reaches into his pocket*.

Hammond sent me this letter. S'all I got.

It don't tell you much but –

CHARLIE. Thank you.

Why don't you go somewhere else. Start over.

NEWLOVE. Can't leave my ma.

'Sides. Where'm I gonna go? If there's one thing you can say about Henry Newlove, it's that he's always right where he's sposed to be.

***

In her bedroom, VICTORIA *continues*.

VICTORIA. I have spent my life cleaning up their mess. No more. I will not have my family cost me my place in the Kingdom of Heaven. Eddy must pay the consequences.

GOD. WHY DO YOU WANT TO ENTER THE KINGDOM OF HEAVEN?

VICTORIA. Is that a trick question? So I can have everlasting peace.

GOD. I DON'T BELIEVE YOU.

VICTORIA. So I can be by your side and –

GOD. TRY AGAIN.

VICTORIA. So I can see my husband again.

GOD. BETTER.

VICTORIA. Albert. My dear Albert. I know he is there. Have you seen him, Lord? Does he look good? Has he asked about me?

I miss him so much.

GOD. AFTER TWENTY-SEVEN YEARS? YOU MUST BARELY REMEMBER HIM.

VICTORIA. How can you say that?

GOD. WHY DO YOU WANT TO SEE HIM AGAIN?

VICTORIA. Because I miss him.

GOD. I DON'T BELIEVE YOU.

VICTORIA. Because I miss his laugh, his wisdom.

GOD. TRY AGAIN. WHY D'YOU WANT TO S–

VICTORIA. Because I miss the way he pleasured me! Alright? Are you happy? I miss the way he made me feel. I miss his lips his hands his tongue the way he touched me the way we touched each other and yes you're right I barely remember the shape of his face or the sound of his voice but I remember that feeling, oh yes I remember that feeling and you took it away from me because you're a cruel and wicked God.

And now all I want is to feel that again in paradise.

To live without touch is an ache.

You know ever since I heard these rumours
About Prince Eddy.

I can't stop

Thinking about it.

About what exactly do they do when they're together. In those rooms.

I lie awake in my bed and I try and imagine my grandson in that house. I imagine him walking up a dark staircase, into a soft, red room and a boy is waiting for him a soft blond boy he has been scrubbed clean his skin is red raw from the bristles and my grandson puts some money on the table and then the boy gets started, started with his hands at first and then his mouth

And I imagine that it feels

I will not sin again. My grandson will pay for his crimes and Albert and I will be reunited.

Thank you. You can go now.

Pause.

GOD. VICTORIA?

VICTORIA…?

VICTORIA. I'm not listening.

GOD. YOU KNOW WHAT YOU HAVE TO DO, DON'T YOU?

***

The stables.

SOMERSET. I'm sorry.

I've thought about it but

Thank you for the offer but I can't go to France right now.

EUSTON. Podge –

SOMERSET. I have things to do here. The stables.
Responsibilities. I can't just up and –

You can go back to His Highness and tell him. Thank you
but no. I'm not leaving.

EUSTON. Jesus, Arthur, think about it. If you don't leave. The
police will come. You will leave in handcuffs, and then you
will be tried, very publicly, at the Old Bailey in front of what
will almost certainly be a full complement of the press.

The letters between you and this boy. They will be all over
the newspapers.

Your parents, your brothers, they will be disgraced.

I don't want to see that happen to you. Nobody wants to see
that happen, old thing, so just –

Take the way out, eh?

SOMERSET. I'll call their bluff. Then. I'll call their bluff and
tell the whole world everything.

EUSTON. Come on –

SOMERSET. I'll say that I saw Prince Eddy there, I'll go to the press if I have to.

EUSTON. Think about what you're saying. Victoria is old. The Prince of Wales is fat and unhealthy. Eddy will be king before long. How many newspapers do you think will print such a thing? Based on nothing but hearsay?

Listen

It won't be so bad. I hear France can be a very welcoming place to live.

SOMERSET. I won't know anyone. My whole life is here.

This is nonsense. It's not fair.

Thirty-five years. Thirty-five years of doing what I'm told, at school, at home, in the army, always doing exactly what's asked of me.

Arthur Somerset the good boy, Arthur Somerset the dependable lad always does the right thing old Podge oh yes –

And then the first time I don't.

The first time I

It's not fair.

EUSTON. Podge

SOMERSET. It's not	EUSTON. You went to this
It's not fair it's not fair	place!
it's not fair it's not fair	Do you know the mess
it's not fair it's not fair	you've caused for me and
it's not	William?

Fair

EUSTON. All things considered, it could be a lot worse.

SOMERSET *accepts his fate*.

SOMERSET. When would I be able to come back?

But, of course, EUSTON *doesn't answer.*

EUSTON. There's one caveat. They'll let you go but only if you promise to say Prince Eddy was never there. You never saw him there and you made it all up.

Say it back to me.

Beat.

Please, Arthur. Say it.

SOMERSET. Prince Eddy was never there.

***

GOD. ARE YOU READY VICTORIA?

TO SEE YOUR FAMILY'S FUTURE.

VICTORIA. I –

GOD. CLOSE YOUR EYES FOR ME.

She does.

Three… two… one…

VICTORIA. Oh!

And suddenly, a future flashes before her eyes.

I see… my grandson being arrested… he's behind bars… he looks ashamed…
His face on every newspaper…

GOD. YES

VICTORIA. I see… crowds of people shouting… rioting in the streets
…a rabid horde storming the gates of the palace…

GOD. WHAT ELSE?

VICTORIA. I see my family… running through corridors…
bullet holes in the kitchen wall…
No… no!

GOD. AND AFTER?

VICTORIA. Revolution… .the country in crisis… chaos… chaos… chaos!

GOD. AND YOU, VICTORIA

YOU FOREVER CURSED TO BE THE LAST OF YOUR
LINE THE FINAL QUEEN OF BRITAIN THE ONE WHO
LOST IT ALL

VICTORIA. No I can't bear it. Show me no more!

It stops.

GOD. DO YOU UNDERSTAND?
THIS IS WHAT WILL COME TO PASS IF YOU DO NOT
PROTECT PRINCE EDDY.

***

St Paul's Police Station.

ABBERLINE. Charlie Swinscow. What do we owe the pleasure?

CHARLIE. I came to give you this. It's a letter Hammond sent
to Henry Newlove.

ABBERLINE. Well that's very useful –

CHARLIE *doesn't hand it over.*

CHARLIE. This gets me off the hook right? I've done enough
to help you?

ABBERLINE. If it's good info. Absolutely.

CHARLIE. Henry too? This keeps us both out of handcuffs?

ABBERLINE. You have my word.

ABBERLINE *nods.* CHARLIE *hands over the letter.*
ABBERLINE *reads it.*

HAMMOND. 'Dearest Henry

Sorry I'm only just writing now. I rather left you in the lurch,
I feel, disappearing like that. Ah well. Life is full of little
let-downs, isn't it?

I'm sitting here, staring at the sea, waiting for my big
adventure.

Our generous benefactors have promised me passage to
America, all expenses can you believe. The life of luxury for
Mr Charles Hammond, oh yes. The least they can do.

I'm sorry I couldn't manage a ticket for you but I suppose I'm just not that good at haggling. I won't spend too much time worrying, because I know you'll be fine. You always are.

My passage is booked for a week on Tuesday. Until then, I'm lying low.

I'll send you a postcard.

H.'

HANKS. 'I'm sitting here. Staring at the sea.'

ABBERLINE. I know. But he don't say where. He don't say what sea, so

HANKS goes digging around on his desk and pulls out a small black notebook. He flicks through it.

HANKS. At the Public Record Office, I couldn't find anything on Hammond, 'cept his mother's birth certificate, I made a note of the registered address. Here we go.

Thirty-Two Castle Road, Portsmouth. Portsmouth's got a sea, right?

ABBERLINE. Hanks, you're a fucking genius! Somerset can wait.

When's the next train from Waterloo?

***

GOD. ARE YOU READY TO SEE A DIFFERENT FUTURE?

ONE WHERE PRINCE EDDY WALKS FREE.

WHERE YOU DO ALL IN YOUR POWER TO MAKE THIS GO AWAY.

VICTORIA. How does this future remember me Lord?

GOD. WHY, AS THE EMBLEM OF AN AGE.

ARE YOU READY CHILD?

VICTORIA. Show me.

And suddenly ANGELS *start to sing. They sing a song familiar, and beautiful and comforting, and rapturous. Something that pierces her very soul. And as they do so…*

VICTORIA *is shown her future. She is shown the way that future culture will talk about her. Will represent her.*

Perhaps she sees a clip from the 2010's ITV show Victoria.

Popular actress of the twenty-first century Jenna Coleman declares her love for Tom Hughes, playing Prince Albert. VICTORIA *gasps.*

What is this? Is that… is that supposed to be me? And Albert! Dear Albert!

Her GOD *smiles and the* ANGELS *sing and more of the future flashes in no particular order and filling her eyes are Anna Neagle in* Victoria the Great, *Emily Blunt in* The Young Victoria, *Judi Dench in* Mrs Brown, *Judi Dench in* Victoria & Abdul, *Victoria Hamilton in* Victoria and Albert, *animated Imelda Staunton in* The Pirates! Band of Misfits. *And then flickering flashing the covers of books and magazines, academics giving lectures on the Victorian Age, students learning about Victoria, politicians talking about the Victorian Age, the name Victoria Victoria Victoria Victoria Victoria Victoria Victoria Victoria Victoria Victoria Victoria Victoria Victoria Victoria Victoria Victoria ringing throughout culture, politics and history. She soaks it in! She soaks it all in!*

GOD *(as she watches)*. DO YOU SEE HOW THEY LOVE YOU REMEMBER YOU CELEBRATE YOU AND WHEN THE END FINALLY COMES WHEN IT IS TIME FOR MANKIND TO EAT THE HORSES AND TURN THE SHOTGUN ON ITSELF THERE WILL STILL BE ONE OF YOU ON THE THRONE BECAUSE THEY NEED YOU THEY NEED YOU LIKE THE AIR THEY BREATHE

VICTORIA. It's all, they are all

Magnificent!

GOD. THEY LOVE YOU

VICTORIA. Yes!

The same moment, in Portsmouth, we hear a knock on the door in the middle of an evening. CHARLES HAMMOND *puts down his book and opens the door.*

Two MEN *are standing there. One is holding a short length of rope.*

I will do it

MAN. You Charles Hammond?

HAMMOND. Wh… who wants to know?

VICTORIA. I will do it Lord I will protect my son I will protect my grandson I will save my people from themselves.

The MEN *barge into the room and grab* HAMMOND.

Do you absolve me for what I am about to do?

HAMMOND. Now hold on –

GOD. OF COURSE I ABSOLVE YOU!

MAN. Let's make this easy

VICTORIA. Do you absolve me?

HAMMOND. Now… now listen fellas please, I don't know who you think I –

GOD. OF COURSE I ABSOLVE YOU!

The rope is round HAMMOND*'s neck. He is dragged off.*

VICTORIA. Do you absolve me?

GOD. OF COURSE I ABSOLVE YOUUUUU!

As the life is choked from HAMMOND, *the* ANGELS' *song gets louder and louder and louder it gets so loud that it is EVERYTHING and then*

Silence.

Her God has left.

And it is just, VICTORIA.

Breathless and alone.

VICTORIA. Oh.

My.

VICTORIA *leaves*.

Everything is very quiet.

EMILY*'s stew is still bubbling away in the corner.*

EMILY. So there's this maggot. Right.

This little, disgustin, maggot. Burrowin his way through something soft and juicy.

And if by some miracle it could somehow speak English it'd be sayin something like –

MAGGOT. I am hungry
I want to eat
Nom nom nom
Now I am full
I don't want to eat.

Now I am hungry
I want to eat.
Nom nom nom.

Now I am full again. I don't want to eat.

Now I am hungr–

EMILY. Everything it ever wants, it gets. What a life. The maggot burrows its way through the only home it's ever known, the bulging leaking left eyeball of the rotting corpse of Mr Charles Hammond.

HAMMOND. *Big skies. Big American skies.*

ABBERLINE. Jesus fucking Christ. We're too late again.

HANKS *picks up a suicide note from the bedside table.*

Suicide note. 'Sorry fer what I done.

Forgiv me Lord.

Hamond.' Spelt wrong.

This look like his handwriting to you?

HANKS. Perhaps you can use this to compare.

He passes him a file.

EMILY. There is a world in which this is the moment in the story where the intrepid police officers crack the case.

ABBERLINE. Hanks where did you find this?

EMILY. Where a stroke of genius gets them all the evidence they need –

HANKS. I noticed a mark on the floor where the bed had been moved, see, and when I looked underneath –

ABBERLINE. The bastard kept records

HANKS. Names, dates. Anyone who ever went to Cleveland Street. When they went there. What they did.

EMILY. A world in which good triumphs and justice is served and Charlie and Emily Swinscow live long happy lives free of trauma and heartbreak

ABBERLINE. This is the whole thing. Right here.

EMILY. But it is not this world.

HANKS. Probably kept it as collateral.

ABBERLINE. Not much good to him now if it was. Some of these names. Politicians. Judges. Clergymen. And –

EMILY. Because then of course he sees the name

ABBERLINE. Stone me.

EMILY. He sees what he's been up against.

He starts to laugh.

HANKS. Sir? What's funny.

He passes him the file.

Is this real?

What do we do with this?

ABBERLINE. I think it's time to take this to the bosses, don't you?

***

EMILY *looks at her Willow pattern plate.*

EMILY. Do you know, I've always hated the ending to this story.

The dead couple and the gods turning them into birds.

Because after everything they've been through, they don't want to be turned into birds, do they? They don't want to be birds.

Why couldn't the gods have turned them back into themselves, back in their little blue house on the island.

Why couldn't they have stopped it happening to begin with? Wouldn't that have made a lot more sense?

***

Scotland Yard. The COMMISSIONER *has the case file.*

COMMISSIONER. Well well, Abberline, I see you've been busy.

ABBERLINE. We certainly have. Constable Hanks here has been invaluable.

HANKS. Thank you, sir.

COMMISSIONER. But looking over this file, I'm not sure that there's much of a case to be made here at all.

Beat.

HANKS. Due respect, but how can you say that?

ABBERLINE. Hanks –

HANKS. Some of those names. And we still don't who was bankrolling it.

COMMISSIONER. Looks like a dead-end to me.

HANKS. If you just give the inspector here more time.

ABBERLINE. No, no. I agree with the commissioner.

Beat.

HANKS. Sir?

ABBERLINE. There's no point wasting valuable police resources any further.

COMMISSIONER. There's also the issue of these telegraph boys Newlove and –

ABBERLINE. Swinscow, sir. Charlie Swinscow.

COMMISSIONER. I hear one of them might be talking to the newspapers. Seem to me like a couple of fantasists. Liable to say all sorts.

HANKS. No that's not what –

COMMISSIONER. I'd like us to nip that in the bud. Charge them both at once.

ABBERLINE. I'm not sure that's necessary sir. The boys –

COMMISSIONER. Have confessed to a crime, Inspector.

ABBERLINE. Right you are. Absolutely.

COMMISSIONER. So you'll bring them in, post-haste?

Beat.

ABBERLINE. Fine.

HANKS. Sir –

COMMISSIONER. I'm sure they'll receive light sentences, so long as they're cooperative. Bring them in and we can consider the matter closed.

That'll be all gentlemen. Thank you.

ABBERLINE. Thing is, the constable and I, well, we've seen and heard things – names – in the course of this investigation that some people might want us to forget.

It'd be an awful shame if some of those names got leaked to the papers.

COMMISSIONER. What do you want, Abberline?

ABBERLINE. Well to put it bluntly.

I want my reputation back.

The Whitechapel Report. It gets buried. Leave the Ripper case open. My little mistake, such as it was, is never mentioned.

I get full retirement, I'm not leaving under a cloud.

COMMISSIONER. Anything else?

ABBERLINE. Yes. Constable Hanks here gets a promotion to detective.

HANKS. No, sir –

ABBERLINE. It's alright, you deserve it, lad. You're a natural.

***

CHARLIE. What happens? When this is done.

EMILY. We get on with things. You go back to work.

CHARLIE. Not the Post Office.

EMILY. Somewhere else then.

CHARLIE. Where.

EMILY. Wherever you want. What would you wanna do if you could do anything?

CHARLIE. I dunno. A shop probably.

EMILY. Oh yeah? What would you sell?

CHARLIE. Don't matter.

EMILY. 'Don't matter', course it matters.

CHARLIE. No. I just. I like the idea. Opening up. Customers. Name on the door. A shop and upstairs a few rooms. Not rented. Owned.

EMILY. Who would you live with?

CHARLIE. Someone nice.

***

The pub.

ABBERLINE. What? Don't gimme that look.

HANKS. You gave up the case, just like that.

ABBERLINE. What case? Hammond's dead, Somerset's absconded.

HANKS. The names in that file –

ABBERLINE. You wanna go march into the palace and handcuff the prince. Be my guest.

Beat.

HANKS. What I don't understand. If they want all this to go away why prosecute the boys?

ABBERLINE. Best guess, our dear commissioner's had someone whispering in his ear. Make an example of them. Send a message.

HANKS. What message?

ABBERLINE. Don't. Fucking. Talk.

Beat.

HANKS. We promised Swinscow that if he cooperated –

ABBERLINE. All things considered –

HANKS. You gave your word

ABBERLINE. it could be a lot worse.

Don't look so glum, Luke. We got what we needed out of this. We put a shift in and we did our work and we got the reward. That don't happen very often.

This is the best-case scenario, this right here.

HANKS. Not for Charlie Swinscow.

ABBERLINE. Yeah well, that was always gonna be the case.

***

EMILY *checks her stew.*

EMILY. Nearly ready.

There's a knock on the door. It makes her jump.

Knock knock knock.

There are few things more violent in this world than a knock on the door in the middle of the –

HANKS *enters.*

Constable. It's late

HANKS. I'm sorry, I'm so sorry but you have to go.

EMILY. What you talking about.

CHARLIE *enters.*

HANKS. Get Charlie, pack your bags, you have to go, now. There is an arrest warrant out for him and this time there'll be no coming home.

EMILY. No, no –

He did everything you said –

Why are you telling us this?

HANKS. Just get him out of here. They'll be here tomorrow.

I'm sorry. I just. I wanted to warn you.

He leaves.

CHARLIE. Mum?

EMILY. Pack your things. Pack your things and take the canvas tent. And go camp out on foreshore. I'll meet you down there when I've got enough money for a train ticket.

Charlie GO!

***

CHARLIE *runs to the foreshore.*

EMILY *runs across town, to Barwell's office.*

She hammers on the door.

EMILY. Mr Barwell! Mr Barwell please open up something's happened! Mr Barwell!! Mr –

But the politician's not there.

He's not fucking there because two hours ago he opened a telegram from the person he admires most in the world saying

GLADSTONE *appears, in all his grandeur.*

GLADSTONE. Fancy joining me for dinner?

Yours, William Gladstone, Leader of the Opposition

I have a personal favour to ask.

You've submitted an urgent question to the speaker for Monday's session about a police investigation into this house on –

BARWELL. Cleveland Street. Yes.

GLADSTONE. I'd like you to withdraw it.

BARWELL. Mr Gladstone. There's clearly been a cover-up – They're shutting down the investigation.

GLADSTONE. You may be unaware, but Scotland Yard recovered a list of clients from the house of the unfortunate Mr Hammond the brothel keeper.

On that list

Are friends of yours and mine.

BARWELL. I. I didn't know that.

GLADSTONE. That list going public would be catastrophic for our election chances.

We will say goodbye to any chance of home rule, extending the franchise… and of course, housing reform, which I know is close to your heart.

BARWELL. This country needs to change Mr Gladstone.

GLADSTONE. Of course it does. But change cannot be rushed. Not with an Englishman, anyway.

The Englishman is born with the unshakeable belief that the way things are must be the way that things have always been, and since he is English and the English do things properly, he thinks that the way things have always been must be the way things are supposed to be as well.

And so they must at all costs stay the same.

Do you follow?

BARWELL. Uh…

GLADSTONE. Baby steps Mr Barwell! Baby steps.

If you hope to stir up thoughts of revolution and republicanism with this little scandal, you are setting yourself up for a grave disappointment. Take it from me, my boy.

We can do so much more if we get into power. But first, we must get into power.

***

Emily's kitchen table.

EMILY. Thank you for coming, sir. They promised us flat-out that if he cooperated he wouldn't see the inside of a cell again and yet –

BARWELL. I'm terribly sorry for your trouble Emily.

Truly, I am.

But I've got myself up to speed on the specifics of Charlie's case.

And I really feel that it's better for everyone if he comes forward.

Beat.

EMILY. I don't understand.

BARWELL. He can't live a life on the run.

If they catch up to him, and he doesn't cooperate, I'm told the boy will be given the full sentence of five years' hard labour.

EMILY. Five years –

BARWELL. But if he comes forward, if he comes quietly, he'll only do six months.

EMILY. Six months. In Newgate.

BARWELL. That's their offer and I think, in the circumstances, it's a good one.

EMILY. I don't understand.

BARWELL. There is a lawyer called Mr Newton who is willing to represent the lad, pro bono.

EMILY. Why would he do that?

BARWELL. But first we need to find him.

EMILY. I don't know where he is.

BARWELL. Emily –

EMILY. I don't know where he is.

Beat. BARWELL *takes out a pouch of money.*

BARWELL. It's hoped you'll accept this as some. Compensation.

EMILY. What's this? A month's rent? You think I'm giving up my son for a month's fucking rent.

BARWELL. It's not a month's rent.

It's a downpayment for the lease on this property.

Pause.

EMILY. What are you talking about?

BARWELL. The Borough of Bermondsey would like to purchase this flat for you. And Charlie.

It would be yours.

No more worrying about the rent. No more living week to week.

EMILY. No no no don't offer me that –

BARWELL. A roof. For the rest of your life.

EMILY. I said don't offer me that!
How can you come here and offer me that?

Who are you?

What am I supposed to say?

You miserable fucking gods turn me into a fucking bird
I don't want to be a bird I didn't ask to be a bird but

of course

Of course

Of course

you're gonna do it anyway.

***

Bermondsey Beach. The Thames laps against the foreshore.

EMILY. The light on Bermondsey Beach at this time of the
morning

CHARLIE. Did you find the money?

EMILY. Oil in the water.

How'd you sleep?

CHARLIE. Rough.

EMILY. Poor lamb.

Pause.

CHARLIE. Wine.

EMILY. What?

CHARLIE. That's what shop I'd like to run, I reckon. A wine
merchant.

EMILY. You don't even drink wine.

CHARLIE. I was thinking 'bout it last night and I thought about
how bad Dad smelt –

EMILY. God he stank, bless him.

CHARLIE. And I'm not sure I'm ready for that. So then I figured, wine.

It don't smell too bad, and people are always happy to be buying it. And the shops always look nice

Nooks and crannies

EMILY. I can see it. Wine. You in a nice apron. Maybe a –

Unnoticed, ABBERLINE *has entered.*

ABBERLINE. Charlie Swinscow –

CHARLIE. Ma?

EMILY. No. Hold on –

You said you'd give us a minute.

ABBERLINE. Come over here son.

EMILY. Please. Just a few more minutes.

CHARLIE. What's going on?

ABBERLINE. You're under arrest for gross indecency.

CHARLIE. What's he talking about.

EMILY. I'm sorry

ABBERLINE. Come easy now son.

CHARLIE. How did they find me?

EMILY. I'm so sorry.

CHARLIE. How did they find me?!

ABBERLINE. Turn around

I said turn around.

EMILY. Just do what he says Charlie.

ABBERLINE *cuffs him.*

CHARLIE. Mum? You told them where I
I was?
no I can't, you told them where I was,
I don't wanna go, I don't,
I don't wanna go, get off me,
why, please, don't,
I don't wanna go,
I don't wanna go,
I don't wanna go

EMILY. Look at me. Look at me.
It's alright
Don't hurt him
I'm sorry
It's okay
I promise
Please
Don't hurt him
It's okay
Love I love you

EMILY. Do what they say.

Do exactly what they say and you'll be home in six months. Six months.

That's not long. Okay?

Six months and everything will go back to normal.

They take him away.

She breaks.

Time passes.

The stew is still bubbling away.

EMILY *tastes it.*

Nods.

It's finally ready.

Twelve years later.

It is 1901.

And then she gets a letter. And it's him. And he's asking for a visit and so she makes a stew

and she waits

and she waits

and she –

CHARLIE *is standing in the doorway. He's older.*

You came

I didn't think

CHARLIE. Said I would

EMILY. I know but

It's great to see you. It's really great to see you. God look at you. You look. You're a man.

Will you come in?

CHARLIE. I don't know.

EMILY. You're gonna come all this way and you're gonna stand in the doorway. Don't be silly.

Pause. He doesn't move.

Okay. That's fine.

I don't know what to. I want to give you a hug. Can I –

She moves towards him. He withdraws.

It's like a bullet to the heart.

She brushes his hair with her fingers instead.

Look at that. You've a bit of grey already, like your / father

CHARLIE. You've a lot.

She touches her hair self-consciously.

EMILY. I made. Food.

It's finally ready if you're / hungry

I made it specially.

CHARLIE. No. No thank you.

Silence.

EMILY. Are you sure?

CHARLIE. If I come in.

EMILY. Yeah.

CHARLIE. Can we just not say anything for a moment.

EMILY. Sure.

He comes in. Silence.

Are you sure you won't eat something. Why don't we sit down?

CHARLIE. I'm not staying.

EMILY. You can stay as long as you like. I thought after all this time we might eat together. And talk. Like when you were little.

Silence.

CHARLIE *notices the plate on the wall.*

CHARLIE. Still got that then?

EMILY. My Willow pattern. Of course! Pride of place.

She takes it down. Passes it to him.

I never use it, only for looking.

He stares at it. And suddenly he doesn't want to hold it any more.

You remember the / story

CHARLIE. Take it back.

EMILY. It's alright you can look.

CHARLIE. Please take it back –

He passes it back to her a little bit too quickly and the plate falls and

Smashes. They both freeze.

EMILY. Don't. Don't worry.

CHARLIE. Sorry.

EMILY. It's fine.

CHARLIE. I'm

EMILY. No harm done.

She picks up the pieces. A little heartbroken.

CHARLIE. I'm sorry. I.

This ain't how I thought this would go.

It doesn't feel the way I thought it would.

EMILY. Why don't you sit down?

CHARLIE. There is a person in my life a very good person

And they convinced me to come.

EMILY. I'm glad they did.

CHARLIE. But now I'm here

EMILY. I did the best for you in the world we were given. I want you to know that.

If you want to be angry with me you can.

But it seems to me

That blaming me don't seem to solve anything.

CHARLIE. Who should I blame then?

EMILY. Well could start with the horse that kicked your father and go from there.

Pause.

She heads over the hob and ladles out two bowls of stew. She puts them on the table.

You know what. I'm gonna dish up because it's ready and it's good it's good meat and it shouldn't go to waste and I know you must be hungry. I'm gonna dish up a bowl for me and I'll do a bowl for you and you can eat it if you want.

CHARLIE. No thank you.

EMILY. Please.

Come on.

Have a spoonful.

Please.

Please eat with me Charlie.

Please.

Come on.

Charlie.
Eat with me.
Just eat with me.
Please.
Please eat with me.
Have dinner with me.
For five minutes.
Eat with me.
Eat with me.
Please.
Charlie.
Eat with me.
Eat with me.
Eat with me.
Please just.
Sit down.
Have some.
Please.

Eat with me.
Eat with me.
Eat with me.
Eat with me.
Eat with me.
Eat with me.
Eat with me.
Eat with me.
Eat with me.
Eat with –

Suddenly, the sound of church bells intrudes from the street outside.

Bong

Bong

Bong

Bong

What is that d'you think? A wedding.

CHARLIE. You ain't heard?

EMILY. No what.

CHARLIE. The Queen died. This morning. S'all anyone's talking about.

EMILY. You're not serious.

Well. I sort of thought that was one of those things that might never happen.

Beat.

In the summer of eighty-seven me and your dad took you down to watch her Jubilee. Do you remember? They had the flags, and the lemonade stands, and the big brass band and everyone was cheering and singing and there were so many people, and we got into the crowd right as she came down the Mall, you remember, and

You were so excited to see her.

The sun was so bright.

CHARLIE. I do.

I remember that.

I think. I'm sorry.

I'm gonna go.

EMILY. No.
Don't go.
Please d–

CHARLIE. I'll see ya.

He leaves.

She watches the space where he once was.

She collapses in on herself.

But then, like she always does, she recovers.

She sits down at the table, picks up a spoon.

EMILY. Well.

God save her then.

Black.

A Nick Hern Book

The Flea first published in Great Britain as a paperback original in 2023 by Nick Hern Books Limited, The Glasshouse, 49a Goldhawk Road, London W12 8QP, in association with The Yard Theatre

Cover photography: Camilla Greenwell; concept: Kia Noakes

Designed and typeset by Nick Hern Books, London
Printed in Great Britain by Mimeo Ltd, Huntingdon, Cambridgeshire PE29 6XX

A CIP catalogue record for this book is available from the British Library

ISBN 978 1 83904 276 8

www.nickhernbooks.co.uk/environmental-policy

www.nickhernbooks.co.uk

facebook.com/nickhernbooks

twitter.com/nickhernbooks